The Other Side of the World

Memoir of a Young Man's Year in Vietnam

<u>Dean Moss</u>

The quotes used within this book have been paraphrased by the author
and are accurate to the extent of the author's recollection.

The bulk of the photographic images in this book are from the author's private
collection. Other images used are from uncopyrighted public domain sources.

Order this book online at www.trafford.com
or email orders@trafford.com

Most Trafford titles are also available at major online book retailers.

Print information available on the last page.

ISBN: 978-1-4269-0025-9 (sc)
ISBN: 978-1-4269-0026-6 (hc)
ISBN: 978-1-4269-0027-3 (e)

Trafford rev. 08/26/2023

www.trafford.com
North America & international
toll-free: 844-688-6899 (USA & Canada)
fax: 812 355 4082

Contents

Forward

The Other Side of the World is a chronicle of my experiences in Vietnam from May 1968 to May 1969. It was written nearly forty years after the occurrence. My audiotapes and three hundred twenty-four handwritten letters to my new wife during that year were my primary source of information. I have also included many personal remembrances – some of which are still vivid while others are admittedly hazy after four decades.

This is a collection of happenings – much like a diary – that doesn't contain a plot. The events described in this book were seen through my eyes as a twenty-year-old young man who was thrust into an alien and hostile environment with minimal preparation. It contains factual accounts of my experiences, involvement and perceptions of a war. It is not meant to be self-serving but rather to tell a story.

The inclusion of humor within this manuscript is in no way intended to take away from the seriousness of the war itself. Footnotes were added to expound on a detail learned later than at the time of my experience.

I realize that every Vietnam veteran has his or her own story – *The Other Side of the World* is mine. I'm forever grateful for the sanctity afforded me by being assigned to an airbase that insulated me from many of the war's atrocities – most of my fellow servicemen weren't that fortunate.

I've been harboring this memoir within my being for nearly forty years and through encouragement from my family and a co-worker, it has now become words on paper. I'm grateful for their support and thank them profusely.

This is my first attempt to write a manuscript of this magnitude. Rereading my letters and listening to the audiotapes have been enjoyable and have rekindled pleasant and sometimes unpleasant memories. *The Other Side of the World* was primarily written for my sons, my grandchildren and perhaps their children so they might have a better understanding of the person they call "Grandpa."

Dean Moss

Acknowledgement

My sincere gratitude is extended to those individuals, far too numerous to mention, who assisted me in making this book become a reality. Your encouragement and support are heartfelt and have contributed greatly toward the completion of this endeavor.

Dedication

To my bride Barbara

Your patience, loyalty, and love have transcended far beyond my expectations. You have supported me at every level. This is really *our* story since you were a major player during my year in Vietnam.

To my Sons

Both of you have been a source of incredible fulfillment in my life and for whom I hold an immense amount of pride and respect. As military officers, you have served with honor and have been duly decorated for your many achievements.

To my Grandchildren

May your lives be wholesome, noble, and happy. As you read this account, it is my aspiration that you acquire wisdom and deeper understanding of the person you call Grandpa.

To my co-worker Brian

Your accolades persuaded me to delve into this undertaking and, without your encouragement, this book would have remained unwritten. For this I am forever grateful.

Chapter 1

"Until Death Do Us Part"

Our Wedding

"If a man and a woman have been married less than one year, he must not be sent off to war or sent away to do forced labor. He must be allowed to stay home for a year and be happy with his wife."

Deuteronomy 24:5

The pastor's words echoed in my head as the reality of the moment began to sink in. The lump in my throat that had barely allowed me to recite the wedding vows relaxed slightly as I glimpsed at my beautiful new bride. Barbara looked so stunningly beautiful and happy – to the extent that I hoped our friends and relatives attending our wedding that rainy Saturday night didn't notice that I was on the brink of a major breakdown.

There I was, a naïve young man only a few years out of puberty, in a baggy Air Force uniform, standing at the altar in the role of a groom. My parents were watching their only child marry a young woman he'd been dating for nearly two years.

Amid the celebration and congratulations, there was a well known but unmentioned topic of conversation – in sixteen short days, I'd be leaving for a year-long tour of duty in Vietnam. The whole scenario was so surreal that many times I wondered if it could all be happening. Everything was moving so fast…perhaps too fast.

The conflict in Vietnam had been steadily escalating all during my high school years. The nightly news frequently aired gruesome footage of the fighting, but those conflicts were on the other side of the world and had little significance to this teenager living in Atlanta. However, the horror of war came crashing home on August 25, 1966 when my former high school ROTC instructor, Sergeant Oliver Dumas[1] stepped on a land mine after being in Vietnam for only two weeks, leaving his three young daughters without a daddy.

After high school, I met and steadily dated Barbara and in three short months we were in love. I enrolled at a local vocational technical school for a two-year study in electronics, which afforded me a temporary student deferment with the Selective Service System[2]. After those two years, I was quickly reclassified as "available" and was considered by the U. S. Government as a prime candidate for the Armed Forces. I didn't fully realize the implication of my status until I received a letter directing me to undergo a mandatory pre-induction medical examination in

---

[1] Sgt. Dumas is listed on panel 10E, line 38 of the Vietnam War Memorial in Washington, DC.

[2] The Selective Service System registered all males between the ages of 18 and 25 for the purpose of drafting them involuntarily in the Armed Services.

preparation for active military service. It looked like a done deal – I was about to be drafted into the Army.

Dad gave me some wise advice, *"Son, you control the situation…don't let it control you."* There was little I could do about my situation so how could I possibly avoid being drafted? The answer hit me like a ton of bricks – join the *Air Force!* My rationale was any duty in the Air Force would be far better than being an Army infantryman even though the enlistment obligation was four years as compared to two years for a draftee. Surely the Air Force wouldn't be that involved in the war. Besides, wasn't it mostly the Army fighting in that conflict somewhere across the ocean?

My decision to join the Air Force delighted the recruiter – something about meeting his quota for the month. I scored well in the screening exams, especially in electronics, and the recruiter said the Air Force was seeking qualified people in electronics. He added that I'd be a "tremendous asset" because I was already trained. I was looking forward to working in an electronics career field and applying my newly acquired knowledge in practical applications.

The night before my report date I said all my good-byes. Barbara and I promised to stay true and faithful to each other during my brief absence[1]. The next morning I reported as instructed only to find that my induction had been delayed by one day. So I returned home and awkwardly repeated the good-byes once again the following night.

On September 19, 1967, I became an active member of the Armed Forces and was whisked away to Lackland Air Force Base

---

[1] My thought process at that time looked upon my Air Force enlistment as a temporary intrusion in my life and things would soon return to normal. I couldn't have been more wrong.

in San Antonio, Texas for basic training. My ROTC training had really prepared me well for a military regiment, making the transition to military life much easier.

Following basic training, I was stunned by my career field placement. Contrary to my recruiter's encouragement about my electronics qualifications, my destiny would be a *weapons mechanic!* When I voiced an objection to my Training Instructor, he replied with amusement, *"Airman, you now belong to the Air Force and you'll do what's best for the Air Force… not what you think is best for you."*

I was assigned to Lowery Air Force Base in Denver, Colorado, where I would embark on a fifteen-week training curriculum to learn about aircraft bombs, rockets, missiles, and guns. I reluctantly embraced this training with a conscientious attitude even though I was completely removed from electronics. I found the subject matter interesting and appreciated the fact I would be working directly with high performance aircraft – a few of my friends from basic training were placed in jobs not associated with aviation. My scores on the weekly block tests were sufficient for me to be listed as an Honor Graduate.

During the eleventh week of training, each class member received orders for his next duty assignment. Contrary to my earlier denial, I realized Vietnam loomed in my future because where else would the Air Force use my career field? But I felt reasonably assured they wouldn't send a student fresh from Technical School to a war zone.

My worst fear was realized. I couldn't believe what I was reading. My orders stated my next permanent duty station would be *Pleiku, South Vietnam!* I was absolutely shocked beyond belief. That couldn't be right…surely there was a mix-up somewhere.

After some futile inquiries, I discovered there was no mistake – I was really being sent to that war on the other side of the world.

That night I finally gathered enough courage to make the dreaded phone calls. I had to wait my turn at the phone booth because a lot of guys were calling home to share their news. The wait afforded me some time to choose the right words to use when I called my parents and Barbara. I mentally rehearsed several ways in which to break the news but decided it was best to be straightforward and hoped they would appreciate my frankness.

My first call was to my parents and to my surprise, they took the news rather well...so it seemed. I suspected they were masking their true feelings on my behalf and probably had already accepted the eventuality of me being sent to war. Either way, I appreciated their apparent composure and understanding[1].

My next call was to Barbara. She too had remarkable composure when I told her. We then spoke a word mentioned only once in our two-year courtship – marriage. Did she really want to marry a person destined for Vietnam? What if the unspeakable happened? Neither of us wanted to make a hasty or foolish decision – we realized that such a matter would require some serious thought so we decided to take some time in which to think things out. I told her I'd call her the following week.

Several days passed and my every waking moment was occupied with the marriage question. Most of my married friends in

---

[1] I later learned Mom really went through a dreadful time knowing her only child would be placed in harm's way. She wrote letters to our Congressman claiming I was a "Sole Surviving Son" which would keep me out of a war zone. To her dismay, for me to have a Sole Surviving Son entitlement, Dad must have served in the Armed Forces and been killed in action.

the Air Force supported a decision of marriage while others believed I'd be a *"damn fool"* to get married under those circumstances. I was torn between practicality and emotion and tried hard to weigh all the factors. After considerable effort, I had to confess that I was in a mental deadlock – I needed to look beyond myself for an answer. That night I prayed for help and was soon blessed with an assurance that brought calmness and a peace of mind.

On Thursday night, March 26, 1968, from a frigid phone booth in Colorado, I asked Barbara to become my wife. Without hesitation she said yes. The previous calmness and peace of mind abandoned me and I laid awake most all night in my bunk staring at the ceiling wondering, *"What in the world have I done?"*

The next few weeks were a blur for me. While Barbara was planning our wedding back home, I purchased a set of unadorned wedding and engagement rings at the Base Exchange for $67.15 and hoped she'd approve[1]. Everything was coming together – our wedding would be on May 4, 1968 in the Chapel at First Methodist Church in Decatur, Georgia.

Before I was allowed to marry, I had to gain the Air Force's consent by attending a mandatory two-session pre-marriage clinic conducted by the Base Chaplain. The permission was documented on an official Air Force Form (ATC Form 548) titled "Notification of Intent to Marry."

My fellow classmate and good friend, Gary Howell from Little Rock, Arkansas agreed to be my Best Man. He was fortunate to have a stateside assignment at Seymour-Johnson Air Force base in

---

[1] The cost of the rings was 70% of my monthly salary.

North Carolina. Gary and his wife Betty would detour to Atlanta on their way to his next station.

Barbara chose her attendants and mailed our invitations. She picked out a beautiful and eloquent wedding gown – a floor length long-sleeved dress with a scalloped neckline and a row of small delicate buttons down the back. Just about everything was ready except for one missing item – me!

I arrived home on April 17, 1968, the Wednesday after Easter, and just seventeen days before the wedding. I was anxious for Barbara to see her engagement ring[1], and when I gave it to her, she loved it! We made an appointment to meet with Rev. Bevel Jones[2] who would be performing the marriage ceremony. Considering our current situation and my forthcoming prolonged absence, he counseled with us for a long while and was candid about the tribulations we could expect.

The wedding would be simple and non-extravagant. The Chapel was an ideal setting with its ornate furnishings and prominent stained glass windows and also because of its center aisle – an absolute must for Barbara. The Sunday before the wedding, Barbara and I joined Decatur First Methodist Church and renewed our baptismal vows.

Rev. Jones said in his most gentle voice, *"You may now kiss your bride."* I carefully drew back the dainty veil that covered Barbara's glowing face and gave her a tender kiss. It was that moment I knew

---

[1]   To this day she still wears that same ring.
[2]   Reverend Jones would later be elected a Methodist Bishop of the Western North Carolina Conference in 1984, a post he held until his retirement in 1996.

I had done the right thing. The pipe organ began to play *The Wedding March* and we recessed down the aisle of the chapel. After our reception in the church's Fellowship Hall, we made a hasty retreat in Dad's car that had been adorned with shaving cream and with cans tied to the rear bumper. Vietnam was as far away from my mind as the country is from Decatur, Georgia.

Our honeymoon was a week's stay near Callaway Gardens located an hour southwest of Atlanta. The timing was ideal for a brilliant display of azaleas in full spring bloom. We stayed at a roadside motel[1] that offered the basic amenities with no frills whatsoever. It was clean and secure and that's all we needed at the moment...except each other and more precious time.

---

[1] Forty-one years later, we returned to that same motel during our anniversary week. The cost per-night had increased 316%!

Chapter 2

"Do Good And Come Home Safe..."

Goodbyes

The dreaded date of May 20, 1968 arrived much too quickly. I was aware of the persona I should be portraying – the courageous soldier going off to defend the homeland, but I couldn't muster the resolve necessary for that façade. On the inside I was a baffled and frightened kid who was way beyond his comfort zone.

Dad drove the car to Atlanta's airport with Mom in the front seat and my new bride and me in the back. We hardly spoke a word – small talk didn't seem appropriate and no one wanted to talk about what really was on our minds. Our thoughts were in sharp contrast to our silence. All of life's adversities seemed so trivial as that situation brought into sharp focus those things that really matter – an important life lesson learned at the young age of twenty.

I checked in my duffle[1] bag and then we walked to the gate. My airfare was purchased at a military rate, so I had to be in uniform while traveling. We arrived at the gate and stood huddled around

---

[1] A "duffle bag" is a large, cylindrical canvas bag for carrying personal belongings used by military personnel.

each other really not knowing what to say. It was an awkward and dreadful moment – we were all masking our emotions with forced smiles. My new bride held back her tears to keep me from becoming distraught, and I was doing the same thing for the same reason. It was so hard saying good-bye – I didn't know how permanent of a good-bye to make it. A year is a long time to be away… but it's shorter than an eternity.

My flight was called, but I lingered until the last moment. Mom hugged me and kissed my cheek. Then she spoke softly into my ear, *"Be safe and take care of yourself. I'll pray for you each day. God bless you, son. I love you."* Fighting back tears, all I could do was nod my head in response. Dad was next – he reached out to shake my hand but I embraced him. Dad had always been an enduring anchor in my life and had earned my unconditional admiration and respect. He spoke to me in an uncharacteristic wavering voice, *"Make us proud, Punkin*[1]. *Do good and come home safe. We love you."* They stepped away to allow Barbara and I to have a private moment.

That was the moment that had caused most of my anxiety. A stifling knot was in my throat so words were near useless. I gave Barbara a lingering hug – she clutched my neck tightly with both arms while standing on her tiptoes. We released our embrace and then I kissed her, *"This isn't a goodbye kiss because I'll be coming back, I promise."* She knew what I meant. She came closer and whispered, *"Never forget that I love you more than anything in the world. I'll write you each day and I'll always be thinking about you."* I choked a reply, *"I know that sweetheart. Try not to worry about me, I'll write you when I can. I love you too."*

---

[1] "Punkin" was Dad's exclusive lifelong nickname for me.

I gave my parents another brief but silent hug. It had to be absolutely horrifying for them to watch their only child leave for a war zone – a moment that I wouldn't really appreciate until much later in life. Mom was especially courageous with her stout composure... not a single tear[1].

I kissed my bride one final time and then walked slowly away from my whole world. The gate didn't have a jet way – passengers walked to the plane on the tarmac and then up some steps and through the plane's doorway. I didn't look back... I *couldn't* look back.

The Air Force serviceman sitting beside me on the plane must have noticed my low spirits because he asked, *"You're headed for 'Nam... ain't you?"* He was either a skillful observer or a lucky guesser. I answered, *"Yeah... is it that obvious?"* He replied, *"Your body language is like a blinking sign."*

He was a sergeant also headed for McChord to pull a second Vietnam tour. He didn't offer a lot of advice about any particular thing – he spoke mostly in general nonspecific terms which annoyed me because that was my first opportunity to find out how things really were in Vietnam... and he was so noncommittal. It made me think he really didn't know... or, worse yet, he <u>did</u> know and didn't want to talk about it.

We arrived at Seattle-Tacoma International Airport and shared a taxi to McChord Air Force Base. We parted company soon afterwards because we were departing on different flights. I checked in at a temporary barracks and was assigned a bunk for my

---

[1] Much later, she confessed to having a long and emotional cry.

brief overnight stay. I scribbled a post card to Barbara letting her know I had made the flight okay. The picture on the postcard depicted the airbase with Mount Rainier looming majestically in the background with its snowcapped summit.

I had a fidgety and restless night – sleep evaded me for the most part and my mind was in a whirlwind. I had to come to terms with myself. I had to admit that, despite the persona I tried to portray, I was frightened out of my wits!

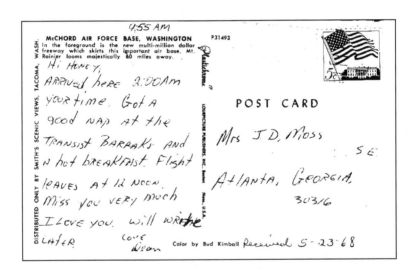

Chapter 3

"To Our Replacements... I'm Sorry."

Port Call

*"The way to develop self-confidence
is to do the thing you fear."*
William Jennings Bryan

My orders read, *"Report to the SEA passenger terminal, McChord AFB,
Washington NLT 1000 hours on 21 May, 1968."* I arrived at the
designated terminal early but the place was already packed with
servicemen from all branches. The room was noisy and smoky with
every seat occupied – many GIs[1] were sprawled out on the floor. A
single television that was mounted on a wall shelf next to the
ceiling was turned on but was mostly ignored.

I joined several soldiers at a check-in line and when I reached
the counter, a staff sergeant barked in a harsh and monophonic
tone, *"Name?"* I told him and he scrolled down the names on the
flight manifest with his finger, found mine, and put a check mark
beside it. Without looking up, he said, *"Leave your duffle bag here, take
a seat and wait until your flight is called. Do not, for any reason, leave the
SEA terminal."* I found out "SEA" was the abbreviation for
Southeast Asia.

---

[1] The term "GI" refers to any enlisted person in the U.S. Armed Forces.
Presumably the initials were derived from "Government Issue."

It took a while, but I finally claimed a vacant seat when its previous occupant took a latrine break. It felt good to sit down away from the lingering cloud of cigarette smoke. I glanced at the television to see a rerun of *The Dick Van Dyke Show* and wondered if that would be my last chance to watch a TV program in a long while… or maybe ever.

The wait allowed me to ponder some things… like what type of military transport aircraft would be used to haul this crowd across the ocean. I was really surprised to find that it was a chartered flight[1] using a commercial carrier – Northwest Orient Airlines. Surely a commercial aircraft wouldn't take us to our final destination in a war zone – we must have an intermediate stop somewhere to change planes. I was wrong in both cases. The itinerary was announced: nonstop from McChord AFB, to Tokyo International Airport and then on to Cam Ranh Airbase in Vietnam. Charter Flight 253A was scheduled to depart at noon.

We boarded the aircraft at 1110 hours, and I made a conscious effort to remember the precise moment my foot stepped off U.S. soil. Inside the plane there were countless rows of six-across seating, separated by a center aisle – the first-class section had been removed to facilitate more passengers. Being in the last group to board, I had to take a center seat between two Army soldiers toward the rear of the airplane. The six flight attendants were all female which again surprised me. We departed on time and our

---

[1] The Military Airlift Command (MAC) contracted with several commercial airlines for passenger service to and from Vietnam, most notably PAN AM and World Airways. These civilian flight crews faced the same risks as their military counterparts in traveling to airports in the major cities in Vietnam. In 1967 the average monthly passenger traffic was in excess of 66,000 servicemen.

nine-hour flight to Japan was underway. Shortly after takeoff, the view out the window was nothing but ocean far below.

The 4,800-mile flight offered me solitude and some time to inwardly reflect on things I never dreamed I'd think about. The thought of me being wounded or maimed was second only to one of my overall survival over the next year – something that a twenty year-old shouldn't have to agonize over. I couldn't get Sergeant Dumas out of my thoughts – he didn't make it past *two weeks*. The fear of the unknown was overwhelming and gut wrenching nearly to the point of nausea. All kinds of thoughts raced through my mind, *"What was it gonna be like? Would I be able to take it? What exactly was it?"*

I looked around at the other soldiers on the plane and noticed very few looked at ease. It was a youthful bunch of GIs – most of whom were my age or younger[1]. It appeared that many were in deep thought and concerned about what was in store for them – just like me. One soldier a few rows behind me was returning for a second tour and was telling war stories to anyone who would listen. His boisterous voice described in gory detail his experiences from his first tour. He seemed to enjoy his advantage but I surmised the bulk of his exploits were a fabrication.

I tried to ease my anxiety by thinking about other matters. My mind raced through topics like it was shuffling a deck of cards and

---

[1] President Johnson's 1965 decision to rely on the draft rather than reserves to provide the manpower for the Vietnam War resulted in a young man's war – 19 years of age became the most common in the field as compared to 26 in World War II. At the height of the conflict, more than sixty percent of Vietnam deaths were 19 to 20 year old draftees.

stopped on a most unlikely subject – something to which I'd never given much thought. I tried without success to rationalize my understanding as to why we were at war in Vietnam. I was ashamed to admit that I didn't have the foggiest of notions. Such matters just weren't important in my young life. I knew we were against the communists, with the enemy occupying the northern half of the country and we, with our allies, were in the south. But as to the reason for the hostilities… I didn't have a clue. I now wished I'd been more attentive to current events.

Frankly, I had become appalled with the network news broadcasts that spewed a nightly stream of war footage into our living rooms[1]. They were constantly competing for viewer ratings so their coverage would often be punctuated with blood and gore in an attempt to showcase the war's atrocities… thinking somehow this would make people want to view their broadcasts over those of their competitors.

In my judgment, the media played a major part in turning public sentiment against the war. The conflict had become intensely unpopular with protestors – mostly on college campuses – demanding an end to the "senseless deaths" of thousands of young men who were forced into the conflict. In one way, I agreed with the protestors – the soldiers weren't fighting because of loyalty or patriotic reasons… they were forced into the war against their will.

---

[1] Known as America's first "television war," Vietnam was the first war for which television was a primary means for providing information to the American public. Critics claimed that TV producers attempted to make their coverage visually dramatic, using short clips aimed at viewers' emotion rather than intellect, resulting in distorted views of the events.

The year 1968 was indeed a tumultuous one filled with hate, rebellion, assassinations, drugs, protest, and defiance. The Selective Service was amassing throngs of eligible young men – those who hadn't dodged the draft by leaving the country[1] – to serve involuntarily in the Armed Forces. The war proved to be the demise of the current president, Lyndon B. Johnson, who refused to accept the Democratic Party's nomination for a second term.

Our in-flight meals were disappointing – mostly cold-cut snack items instead of a decent hot meal. The Army soldier seated next to the window looked like a "Gung-Ho" type of commando – the sort that might sleep in bed wearing camouflage face paint. He was very deliberate to demolish all disposable items from his meal tray including plastic silverware, cups, and napkins. He even extinguished his cigarette by snuffing out the butt into a small, unused container of jelly. I asked him why he did that and he replied, *"I was taught never leave anything that the enemy could benefit from."* Nothing like that was ever mentioned to me.

I really didn't feel the Air Force had adequately prepared me for Vietnam. My only war zone training consisted of becoming qualified with an M-16 rifle and firing an ammo clip in the full automatic mode. I attended some briefings but they were mostly how to prepare a legal will and procedure for granting the Power of Attorney to a spouse. I thought I'd have training on booby traps, land mines, and hand grenades… something to that effect. I didn't

---

[1] An estimated 70,000 draft dodgers fled to Canada by 1972.

even get issued any protective body armor because, *"All of that will be taken care of when you get in-country."*

We arrived at Tokyo International Airport in what seemed to be mid afternoon – my first time ever to be in a foreign country. Flying across the ocean really messed up my time perception – we had flown through seven time zones, and our westerly travel made local time pass more quickly. Somewhere over the Pacific, we crossed the International Dateline, which actually put us into the next day.

The aircraft taxied to an open area of the tarmac well away from any passenger gate. It was announced we would take on a new aircrew and refuel the aircraft, but passengers would not be disembarking. For those who desired, we could go to the top landing of the boarding stairs to get some fresh air, and I was among the twenty or so GIs that did.

Not long afterwards, another military-chartered aircraft landed and taxied to the tarmac adjacent to ours. They too were allowed to stand on the boarding steps and we acknowledged each other with hand waves. Unexpectedly, a lone GI from the other plane ran over to us with a note in his hand. He delivered the message and scurried back. The note read, *"To our replacements: Xin Loi."* I wondered how he knew we were headed to Vietnam and not from… did we look that fresh? The veteran GI aboard our aircraft read the handwritten note and interpreted the message as saying, *"To our replacements: I'm sorry."*

In about an hour, we were again underway on the final five-hour flight. The new flight attendants were all Japanese females –

strikingly attractive women who were constantly smiling and spoke perfect English. They were in sharp contrast with the mundane attendants on the first leg of our journey. Their cheerful personalities were therapeutic and definitely boosted my emotional state. I searched my memory and concluded this was my first encounter with anyone of Japanese origin – Atlanta simply didn't have that many Asians in the 1960s.

As we got closer to our destination, I began to be overtaken with anxiety. Despite being the victim of severe jetlag, sleep was out of the question – I was much too restless. I had a feeling that my life was about to be forever changed in some inexplicable way. This could be a good thing... or it could be my worst nightmare turning into a reality.

Something inside kept telling me to just acknowledge the anxiety and then put it out of my mind. I remembered Dad's astute advice, *"Son, you control the situation...don't let it control you."* Was this situation out of my control? Maybe so...but I could still control my mindset and that's probably half the battle. I closed my eyes and took several deep breaths, trying hard to convince myself everything would be okay. I was unsuccessful... the situation was definitely controlling me at that moment.

Chapter 4

"Contrastingly Serene..."

Vietnam Arrival

*"As a rule, man is more fearful of things he
cannot see than things he can.."*
Julius Caesar

As we approached the Southeast Asia mainland, a male voice announced our arrival via the aircraft's cabin speakers. He said the shoreline would be coming into view on the right side of the aircraft. Most of the two hundred-fifty GIs strained for a view out the small windows for our first glimpse of Vietnam. Many, including myself, were standing in the center aisle peering over heads and backs.

After a short while, a heavily forested and mountainous shoreline appeared out the windows. We could see vivid landmarks that cast long shadows behind the setting sun. I looked intently for any signs of war – troops, explosions, helicopters, smoke, etc. None were visible. The view was contrastingly serene – not at all what I had envisioned Vietnam to look like.

Nighttime had darkened the sky when we landed at Cam Ranh Airbase. The long flight should have made me dreary, but my adrenaline was doing back flips at that point. An Air Force officer dressed in jungle fatigues boarded our aircraft and spoke to us over the cabin speakers. Instead of a greeting, he began to give us robotic instructions about our in-processing procedure once inside the terminal area. Nothing was mentioned about our immediate action to insure our safety from hostile actions… information that

I was keenly anticipating. I wondered if we should run for cover when we reached the bottom of the boarding stairs.

My first introduction to Vietnam was the onslaught of hot humid air that parched my face when I stepped out of the plane's doorway. It was literally like peering into a hot oven – only the relentless heat never stopped. I wondered if I'd ever get acclimated to the Vietnam's vicious weather. Surely so over time… and I had a great deal of it in which to get adapted.

As I descended the stairway, I peered into the darkened areas of the tarmac looking for any unusual happenings, not knowing if I should be ready to take cover. The crowd of servicemen walked timidly in single file to the passenger terminal, a large metal building that looked more like a warehouse.

Looking down, I noticed my shadow on the tarmac…. was it from moonlight? No, an extremely bright light that hung in the night sky like a really high street light was illuminating the airfield and surrounding area. At first I thought it was some sort of searchlight on an aircraft, but I quickly dismissed that idea because whatever was causing the light wasn't moving and was absolutely silent. I later asked the veteran serviceman about the light and he said it was from an illuminary flare[1] tossed from a circling aircraft.

The terminal was brimming with activity – soldiers were crammed in the area either coming or going to places elsewhere. The menagerie was a case in contrast – some GIs were asleep on the concrete floor with heads resting on their steel helmets; some

---

[1] The costly but necessary luminary flares were used extensively throughout Vietnam to better detect enemy activity at night. In 1966, the Department of Defense asked five aerospace companies to explore the feasibility of orbiting an array of mirrors in space to reflect sunlight to Vietnam at night.

were engaged in robust games of poker and wagering money, cigarettes, cameras, and jewelry; some were reading everything from *Playboy* magazines to Bibles... unmindful to the commotion around them.  The area reeked from the hot stale air, body odor, and cigarette smoke[1]. Their seemingly lack of concern of being in a war zone was somewhat comforting – they didn't seem to be uneasy so my anxiety level dropped a few notches.

During in-processing, I had to exchange all of my U.S. currency with the like amount in Military Pay Certificates (MPC) – sometimes referred to as script or "funny money." The new currency was a bit awkward because there were no coins – all  denominations were paper money. Each bill was a different color with print on both sides, and most depicted a portrait of some unknown female figure. MPC was necessary, so I was told, to control inflation in the local Vietnamese economy. How MPC helped that matter was beyond my comprehension at that moment.

I felt awkwardly conspicuous for at least two reasons – I was dressed in my khaki uniform including highly shined shoes that

---

[1] Some smoke had a distinctive sharp, pungent scent that I later identified as marijuana.

broadcasted my neophyte status. Also my one-stripe Airman rank definitely put me in the minority — most of the soldiers in the terminal were significantly higher in rank and appeared to be scruffy battle veterans.

I claimed my duffle bag from a wheeled cart and went directly to the latrine area to change out of my khakis. I felt a little better in my boots and fatigues even though they were still starched from Technical School. There was little I could do about my rank except wait for my promotion to Airman First Class (two stripes) that was due the following month.

My in-country destination was Pleiku Airbase located in the Central Highlands about one hundred-fifty nautical miles northwest from Cam Ranh. My orders had me assigned to the 4th Aero Commando Squadron (ACS), whose primary mission was to  provide close air support to U.S. and other allied ground forces. A fleet of C47 cargo aircraft, the military version of a DC-3, had been modified with three rotating-barrel Gatlin miniguns aimed out of the left side of the aircraft The gunship would orbit a ground target and deluge the area with bullets — *lots of bullets* — in a very short time[1]. I was destined to fly missions with the ACS to keep the miniguns loaded and properly operating — a bit of information I wisely withheld from my family.

---

[1] One minigun could fire at the rate of 4000 rounds per minutes (66 per second!).

I found the next available flight to Pleiku was the following morning at 0800 hours. I then realized that I had no idea of the local time – my wristwatch was still on Atlanta's time. I spotted a wall clock and, to my surprise, my watch was only one hour off… Vietnam was eleven hours ahead of Atlanta[1]. I reset my wristwatch for the local time and thought, *"How bizarre – we were ending the same day that Atlanta was just beginning!"* Indeed, I <u>was</u> on the other side of the world.

I asked a GI working behind a counter what I could do until my flight the next morning. He said I could remain in the terminal area or go to the transit quarters where servicemen routinely lodged for a brief overnight stay. My first inclination was to stay in the terminal because it seemed to offer security, but I was becoming weary and a bed sounded far better than the concrete floor. I asked him the whereabouts of the transit quarters and he said, *"It's across the airfield so you'll need to take a shuttle bus…they run twice an hour but you just missed one."*

With some time to spend, I browsed around the terminal and had my first face-to-face encounter with a Vietnamese. The frail and nonthreatening man was vending foodstuff and beverages from a makeshift stand that I assumed he closed up and hauled away later in the evening. I purchased a lukewarm Coke from the gentleman using my new MPC. He conducted the transaction in silence while crouched in a sitting position.

The elderly man was dressed in a black silken long-sleeved shirt, baggy fatigue pants, and flip-flop sandals. He wore a long thin mustache that drooped down from both corners of his mouth. His

---

[1] Vietnam is in the Indochina Time Zone.

years were readily apparent by the age spots that peppered his complexion. The sight of that feeble man evoked an unexplainable feeling of pity for him.

The shuttle bus arrived ten minutes late and was driven by an A1C[1] who seemed to deplore his assignment. I boarded the bus with my duffle bag and took a seat up front near the driver. I noticed the bus windows were missing but some type of mesh wire screen covered the openings. Besides me, the bus had three other passengers, two of whom were asleep or unconscious – I couldn't tell which. I asked the driver about the screen wire and he answered without taking his eyes off the roadway, *"It's chicken wire… that keeps anyone from tossing a grenade inside the bus. But that chicken wire makes one helluva convenient hanger for a satchel charge."* I agreed with him having no idea what a satchel charge was.

The fifteen-minute commute around the periphery of the airfield was made in silence except for our brief conversation about the chicken wire. As far as I could determine, we were the sole occupants on the roadway – the ever-present flares[2] were illuminating the road far beyond the brightness of the vehicle's headlights. Again, my neophyte mind wondered if the driver was armed. I knew I surely wasn't. The words *"satchel charge"* kept creeping into my thoughts.

---

[1] Airman First Class

[2] A Mark-24 magnesium flare burns for about three minutes at 4,000 degrees and creates two million candlepower intensity. Flares were held aloft by an attached parachute and were in the sky nonstop all night, every night.

The transit quarters was a medium sized building called a hootch that was divided into screened partitions. Each partition had four metal-framed beds, each with a flattened mattress. I was issued a sheet and a pillow at the front desk and was told to claim an unoccupied bed in the farthest partition. The heat was stifling and I wondered why the sheet was necessary.

I heard some loud music coming from within the hootch and found that it was originating from, and I should have guessed, the farthest partition. When I entered the darkened area, I could barely discern the silhouette of a person lying face-up on a bunk near the window – the darkness was disrupted by the occasional red glow of his cigarette. He was listening to an eight-track tape player[1] that blared excruciatingly loud rock music. Enough light from the flares allowed me to stumble around until I found a bunk in the far corner – as far away as possible from the annoying noise. As my eyes adjusted to the darkened room, I saw that my companion was an Army soldier who had completely ignored my arrival. I also noticed a loaded M-16 rifle at his side on the bed.

I unfolded the sheet, spread it over the musty mattress, and stretched out fully clothed on the bunk with the pillow under my head. I didn't undress or remove my boots in case I had to make a hasty exit for some unimaginable reason. I was extremely anxious about the situation and took keen notice of my surroundings not really knowing what was significant and what was a routine occurrence. The eerie shadows being cast from the flares were mesmerizing as they steadily moved up the screened walls in a slow silent cadence.

---

[1]   An eight-track tape cartridge is a closed loop and will replay itself until manually halted.

The stagnant night air was horrendously hot and I was soon clammy with perspiration. To worsen matters, mosquitoes began to feast on my face and arms. I began to slap at the annoying insects at regular intervals and wondered why the pests weren't bothering the other guy. Perhaps the cigarette smoke repelled them... or maybe they were biting him and he was too callous to care. In desperation, I stripped off the sheet from the mattress and laid down on the mildewed mattress with the sheet covering my face and arms.

It was a long time before the Army GI acknowledged my presence. He lowered the volume somewhat and remarked in a flippant tone, *"Hope you like this kinda music... but I really don't give a shit cause it's gonna play all night whether you like it or not!"* I mumbled a reply from under the sheet that I didn't mind the music. I lied.

My first night in Vietnam was filled with trepidation[1]. For the longest time I laid under the sheet in my drenched clothes wishing I could silence the blaring tape player. In an effort to drown out the noise, I placed the pillow over my head... but that didn't last long – the heat was too intense and suffocating. My cynical mind wondered if the tape player was masking distant gunfire. Maybe that was the reason for the deafening music. All sorts of bizarre scenarios raced through my mind and added to my anxiety.

Despite the less than ideal condition of my surroundings, jet lag was catching up with me and I was being overtaken by weariness. Then a frightful thought startled me – I didn't have an alarm clock

---

[1] A total of 997 servicemen were killed within the first 24 hours after arriving in Vietnam. The month I arrived (May 1968), 2,415 casualties were incurred – the most casualties for a single month.

and I couldn't see my wristwatch in the darkened room! What would happen if I overslept and missed my flight? I decided I had no choice but to remain awake overnight... if I could.

I'm still not certain what woke me, but it wasn't quite daybreak yet. I frantically threw back the sheet and looked at my wristwatch. To my relief, it was a little before 0500 hours...so I relaxed a bit longer and began to unconsciously scratch at the whelps created by the mosquito bites. I couldn't believe how hot it was so early in the morning. Then I realized something was different – the room was silent! My first thought was the GI turned off the music during the night but then I discovered I was alone in the partition...the soldier and his music were gone.

I hurriedly collected my belongings and checked out of the transit quarters. The bus was on time and, to my surprise, it was the same driver. I wondered if he had worked all night but I didn't ask him. He didn't acknowledge me in any way – maybe I wasn't as conspicuous as I once thought.

Daylight provided a new perspective of my surroundings. Cam Ranh Airbase was located on a peninsula composed *entirely of sand* – tons of white sand[1]. Many of the roadways and at least one runway used a metal reinforced matting material[2] placed directly on top of the sand to provide a stable and secure surface for vehicles and aircraft. Walking on the sand was difficult because each grain of

---

[1] The sandbar provided the eastern boundary for the crescent Cam Ranh Bay. The sandbar also shielded the bay from the South China Sea and provided a safe harbor for many small fishing boats.

[2] Pierced Steel Planking (PSP) - perforated matting material used for the rapid construction of temporary landing strips.

sand was rounded – much like a ball bearing. For that reason, walkways were necessary and were built using wooden slats that resembled a boat dock.

I arrived back at the passenger terminal to find a much smaller crowd than the night before. The frail Vietnamese man was still there and I wondered if he stayed there all night. I checked the flight schedule and discovered the MACV[1] flight to Pleiku had been delayed due to a mechanical problem, but repairs were being made and the flight would commence shortly.

Following a two-hour delay that hardly described the word "shortly," we boarded the aircraft through the rear cargo door that was hinged at the bottom and, when lowered to the ground, provided a ramp in which people, cargo, and vehicles could enter the aircraft. The cargo bay was packed with what looked liked ammunition canisters strapped to wooden pallets and secured to the floor with large restraining cargo nets. I was among fourteen other passengers, all with full battle regalia. We were seated along the interior wall of the fuselage in nylon-webbed seats that were hinged to the wall.  My seat was well away from the two small windows in the cargo bay so I wouldn't be able to view the landscape during the sixty-minute flight.

---

[1] The Military Airlift Command Vietnam (MACV) flew scheduled flights to thirteen intra-theater air bases using a variety of aircraft but mainly C-123, C47, C130, and C7 cargo aircraft.

I naïvely asked the Loadmaster[1] what type of aircraft we were on and he boastfully replied, *"Airman, you're aboard the best damn aircraft in the Air Force – a C-130 Hercules!"* I thought to myself if that was such a great aircraft, why then did it have mechanical problems.

As we approached Pleiku Airbase, the Loadmaster alerted the passengers that we'd be making a "Corkscrew" landing approach. He said to make sure everyone's lap belt was tight and to basically *"hang on!"* I appreciated the warning… otherwise I'd swear the plane was crashing. The pilot flew the plane high over the airfield – safely beyond the range of any small arms weapon fire. The pilot then banked the C-130 sharply to the left and descended toward the ground in a slow, tight circle, like someone walking down a spiral staircase. At the last moment, he broke out of the spiral and landed on the runway. It was a harrowing experience and, despite the previous warning, one that I was totally unprepared for.

The most noticeable contrast about Pleiku was the cooler temperature[2]. The sky was overcast and the area was wet from a recent rain that made the air thick with humidity. There was an eerie sense of uneasiness – almost like something had just happen-ed or was about to happen[3] and everyone knew it… except me. The Loadmaster asked about the whereabouts of my flak vest and helmet. When I told him I hadn't been issued any battle gear, he

---

[1] The "loadmaster" is a crewmember of a transport aircraft that is in charge of the cargo.

[2] The Central Highlands typically had a moderate climate as compared to coastal regions due to the higher elevation.

[3] The Viet Cong had recently attacked Pleiku Airbase resulting in killing of nine Americans and destroying five aircraft.

replied, *"See about getting some gear as soon as possible."* Suddenly, the incessant heat at Cam Ranh didn't seem all that bad.

I made my way to the 4th Aero Commando Squadron and found the Orderly Room[1]. I reported in and gave a copy of my orders to a Tech Sergeant behind a desk. He looked at my orders and then noticed my lone stripe on my starched fatigue shirt. I knew something was amiss when he sighed, rolled his eyes, and slowly shook his head. I was told to "stand-by" and then I observed a robust conversation beyond my earshot between the Tech Sergeant and a Senior Master Sergeant.

Several times the Tech Sergeant gestured toward me and then slapped my orders with the back of his hand. It looked like a ballplayer disputing the call of an umpire. The conversation ended abruptly with the Senior Master Sergeant making a brief phone call.

With renewed composure, the Tech Sergeant called me aside and said, *"Look, don't take this personal, but we can't use you here. We were expecting a fully trained and qualified Airman, not a trainee straight from Tech School. We're much too occupied with mission priorities to provide you with the necessary training."*

I didn't know how to take that news. Would I be sent back to the states for the "necessary training?" My answer came next, *"We're gonna send you down to Nha Trang. You'll be assigned to the 21st TASS. That's a tactical air support squadron. They've got the time and manpower to train you. There's a flight to Nha Trang departing at 1300 hours today. Have a good tour, son."*

---

[1] An "Orderly Room" is the administrative office of a military unit.

I really wasn't in any position to dispute that decision so I just said, *"Yes sir,"* and I shouldered my duffel bag and exited the room. Once outside, I felt absolutely crushed. That was my first duty assignment and I desperately wanted to make a good first impression... but I failed to make the grade.

With disappointment, I went back to the passenger terminal and found an aeronautical map on the wall. I searched the map for a place called Nha Trang. I finally located it – it was a coastal town an inch above Cam Ranh. My first thought was the dreadful heat – it was late May with the hottest months yet to come.

While waiting for the flight, I scribbled a quick letter to Barbara letting her know that I was okay – and that I wouldn't be stationed at Pleiku as originally told. The letter was short, less than three paragraphs, but the foremost bit of news was that of my wellbeing. I had no idea how long it took for mail to reach Atlanta.

My lack of body armor, especially a steel helmet, seriously daunted me. When and where would I get my gear? I decided I'd be more assertive at Nha Trang and insist an immediate issue. Yeah, right... as if they'll jump through hoops when a one-stripe Airman makes a demand. On second thought, I decided to politely ask and hope for the best.

The flight to Nha Trang was aboard a C-7 *"Caribou"* STOL[1] cargo aircraft. It was a lumbering flight as compared to the C-130, but I

---

[1] Short Take Off and Landing

had a seat near one of several windows in the cargo bay and enjoyed the view tremendously… all the time wondering how safe it was having my face pressed against the window.

Flying at a high altitude allowed me to observe the lay of the land and there was a marked contrast between the central highlands and the coastal region. On one part of our flight, the ground was checker-boarded with what I assumed were fields of rice patties. We passed over a major mountain range just before we began our descent into the coastal valley where Nha Trang was located. Lush vegetation blanketed the landscape and several streams meandered through the green valley.

Not once did I see any signs of a war or conflict – everything appeared peaceful and calm. A thought occurred to me that maybe the pilot chose a route well away from any known areas of conflict or battlefields and that's why everything appeared so serene.

Chapter 5

"Mortar Valley Manor"

Nha Trang Arrival

*"Live as if you were to die tomorrow, learn as
if you were to live forever."*
Mahatma Gandhi

The approach into Nha Trang was from over the ocean and didn't
require the corkscrew descent. My first view of the area was a white

sandy beach[1] just outside
the main gate of the
airbase. As we flew over
the beach, I noticed the
beach was occupied with
people sunbathing and
swimming! *What?...* How
could that be? This is

Vietnam...a war zone! I felt like I was in some type of time warp
or something.

When I stepped off the plane, I was again greeted by the expected deluge of hot air...but I felt considerably safer in the heat
than I did at Pleiku. Nha Trang's Aerial Port wasn't anything like
Cam Ranh's passenger terminal. The area was almost deserted
except for the arriving passengers from my flight. I saw a staff

---

[1] Nha Trang was famous for its tropical pristine beach and, at one time, was
the in-county R&R destination for all of Vietnam.

sergeant who looked as if he might work at the terminal and asked him how to get to the 21st TASS. The sergeant replied, *"No problem... I'll give them a call and most likely they'll send someone to pick you up."* That was something I seldom  experienced in my brief Air Force career – a cordial sergeant willingly assisting an Airman.

He made the call and then said, *"A jeep will be here in about fifteen minutes."* I thanked him and then we chatted during the wait. I just had to ask, *"So, tell me about the beach I saw while coming in. Is it accessible to the military?"* He smiled and replied, *"When security conditions allow it, the beach area is accessible to all Armed Forces Personnel...even to one-striped Airmen!"* I had a feeling I was going to like being stationed at Nha Trang.

The jeep arrived and was driven by another sergeant. I threw my duffle bag into the rear seat and climbed in the front passenger  seat. We drove down an improvised road that was parallel to the flight line. To our left, looking away from the airstrip was a nearby mountain range. At regular intervals along the airbase boundary were guard towers much like that of a prison – only the armed sentries were looking away from the compound.

The closeness of the mountains created some concern for me – it appeared to offer an ideal tactical location for the enemy to launch an assault on the airbase since it overlooked the entire area. I asked the driver, *"Does the airbase ever come under attack?"* He answered, *"Damn right it does… they don't call Nha Trang the 'Mortar Valley Manor' for nothing. Matter of fact, we got hit just last night."* My heart sank and I had to ask, *"Do mortar attacks happen very often?"* He replied, *"Depends… sometimes once a month, sometimes once a week. During Tet, we got clobbered every night!"* I had no idea about the meaning of Tet, but later found out it was a Vietnamese New Year celebration.

During the short drive, I wondered what type of aircraft the 21st TASS flew on its missions. Being a tactical squadron, surely they must fly some type of fighter jet. Hopefully, it was the awesome F4 *Phantom* fighter that I had a passion for. It could be an F-100 *Supersaber* squadron, or maybe the squadron flew the F-105 *Thunderchief.* Regardless, I looked forward to working with any high performance jet aircraft.

When we arrived at the squadron area, I was shocked to find small *propeller-driven* airplanes. Not the massive and powerful World War II era fighters… but diminutive Cessna type aircraft found at most municipal airports back home – except these airplanes carried rocket launchers under both wings. The smaller of the two types of planes was a single engine, high wing tail-dragger. The other was a high wing box-tail with two engines – one engine pulling in the front and the other pushing from the rear. The absence of any jet fighter aircraft was a major letdown – how could these toy airplanes make a difference in the war effort?

I reported to the 21st TASS Orderly Room and they were actually expecting me – they had received a phone call earlier from Pleiku about my transfer. It was late afternoon and their primary concern was finding quarters for me. I was told that, as of the moment, there was no availability in the squadron's barracks and I'd have to stay a while in the transit quarters. My first thought was, *"Not again!"*

Much to my surprise and delight, the transit quarters were not at all like those at Cam Ranh. It was a large open area on the second floor of one of the permanent barracks. The area was filled with rows of bunk beds and lockers. It was bright and breezy and the bunks didn't smell of mildew. I walked around the room and claimed an unoccupied upper bunk – all the lower bunks were already taken.

After an unexpected hot meal at the chow hall, I was more than ready to clean up. I was pretty grungy and hadn't bathed in days. My fatigues were smelly and thoroughly sweat stained. I stripped down to my boxer shorts and, with my toiletries and towel, went to the nearby central latrine facility. As I approached the showers, I heard water running in the open shower bay. I removed my shorts, turned the corner, and entered the shower bay wearing only my dog tags. I was startled to find the shower bay occupied by several *Vietnamese women!* They were fully clothed and doing laundry using water from the showerheads. I sheepishly apologized and backed out of the area, not knowing really what to say or do. They hardly looked up from their chores and that eased my embarrassment somewhat. Maybe I overlooked a shower schedule somewhere... I didn't know. My shower was replaced by an abbreviated wash at a sink.

My second night in Vietnam was an emotional roller coaster. As I lay in my bunk, I could peer through the windows at the flares hanging in the darkened sky. The room was dimly lit by a few overhead bare light bulbs that contributed to the already high temperature, but a nice breeze from the direction of the ocean helped cool down the area and also repelled any pesky mosquitoes. It felt good to be on top of the sheet in my boxers rather than being fully clothed and sweltering under the sheet like I had been the preceding night.

I took a deep breath and closed my eyes enjoying the peace and tranquility of the moment. My body was relaxed but my mind was occupied by thoughts of my new bride. My memory recalled with adoring detail our wedding ceremony and how strikingly beautiful Barbara looked in her wedding gown. I was stricken with the thought that it would be a very long time before I could hold her again. I became overwhelmed with emotion and silently sobbed into my pillow, hoping no one would notice or hear me weeping.

I was recovering from my weak moment when suddenly I was jolted into reality – a nearby explosion shook the whole building! In near panic, I bailed off the bunk onto the floor as another blast rattled the area. With my heart pounding, I was besieged with a sense of helplessness and shear fright – a feeling like no other I had ever experienced! I had fleeting thoughts that I might have a *shorter* longevity than Sergeant Dumas.

After a few moments, I looked around the room and to my utter amazement, saw no concern or panic whatsoever from any of the other tenants. I calmed down a little only to be shaken by a third blast. I slowly came to realize we weren't under an attack, so I collected my wits and tried to walk calmly over to a GI in a nearby bunk who was quietly reading a novel.

I asked, *"What's all the racket about?"* He closed his book with his finger as a bookmark, reached up and removed two earplugs, and replied, *"H&I cannon fire from the Army camp. Starts about this time every night… you'll get used to it after a while."* I had to ask, *"What's H&I anyway?"* He explained, *"It's Harassment and Interdiction[1] … they're really not aiming at any particular target, it's just random firing just to let Charlie know we're still here."* Charlie? Who's that and why would we want to let him know we're here? I thought best to end the conversation before I made a complete fool of myself... but I felt it was too late for that. *"Oh, okay, thanks."* He reinserted the earplugs and resumed reading. Later, I found out "Charlie" was short for "Victor Charlie" the phonetics for Viet Cong, i.e. our enemy.

I returned to my bunk still a bit rattled over the occurrence. I calmed down enough to write a brief one-page letter to Barbara letting her know I had made it to Nha Trang okay. But more

---

[1] Harassment Fire is fire delivered for the purpose of disturbing rest, curtailing movement, and lowering the morale of enemy troops by threat of casualties or loss in material." Interdiction Fire was "fire delivered for the purpose of denying the enemy the unrestricted use of an area or point. H&I accounted for almost 70 percent of all ammunition expenditures in Vietnam and its effectiveness was frequently challenged.

importantly, I gave her my address[1] so she could write me. A letter from her would have been so welcomed at that moment – I would cherish any contact from back home. In my letter, I mentioned the H&I fire and also the fact that the airbase came under a mortar attack the previous night – something I would later regret because it caused undue worry for Barbara.

The H&I fire subsided and once again things got still and quiet. I stretched out on the bunk and rested my head on the pillow, which was still damp from my earlier tears. Before long, I was in a deep sleep – but not for long because another round of H&I startled me. That cycle went on most all night, and by daybreak I was worn out both physically and mentally. I thought to myself, *"Welcome to Vietnam!"*

---

[1]   All mail to and from Vietnam was processed through an Army Post Office (APO) in San Francisco. The five-digit address for Nha Trang was 96205.

Chapter 6

"Did He Say Crotch Rot?"

Indoctrination

> *"Start by doing what's necessary, then what's possible, and suddenly you are doing the impossible."*
>
> St. Francis of Assisi

The next morning I wearily reported back to the squadron and the Orderly Room clerk began my in-processing. I sat in a chair next to his desk as he began filling out a form by asking me questions such as full name, service number, next of kin, and emergency contact information, etc. I couldn't help but notice that he had a small yellow and black ribbon through the top buttonhole of his fatigue shirt. I wondered what that signified but I didn't ask.

Everything was going smoothly until he asked, *"What's your DEROS?"* I replied, *"My what?"* He leaned toward me and slowly repeated, *"Your DEROS... when did you arrive in Vietnam? Your DEROS is the date you'll depart the country.[1]"* I replied, *"I got here the day before yesterday."* He rolled his eyes and stated, *"Whoa, you really are a*

---

[1] DEROS was an acronym for Date of Expected Return from Overseas. It was an innovation of the Vietnam War, and was originally intended to increase morale by letting combat troops know when their tour might end. However, the fixed DEROS was blamed for creating a slackening of effort in anticipation of departure. Whether or not this was so, it was evident that consciousness of the DEROS was an important part in every serviceman's life.

new guy. Your DEROS is 362 days from today on 21 May, 1969." That
date seemed an eternity away.

Next he asked about my blood type. I wondered if that
information would be used for me to donate blood or to *receive*
blood. I told him I had no idea what type of blood I had. He said
disgustedly, *"Look on your dog tags[1], Airman."* I reached under my
fatigue shirt and tugged at my neck chain exposing the two

identical metal dog tags dangling
underneath. Sure enough, "B Pos"
was stamped into my dog tags. The
clerk suggested I get some rubber
edge protectors to lessen the
clanking sounds from the metal tags.

"Why would I want to silence my dog tags?" I asked. His answer was
unsettling, *"To avoid revealing your position if you're trying to hide from the
enemy."*

Next he issued me a ration card[2] that would be used to limit
the purchase of tobacco, alcohol, and big-ticket items such as
cameras, stereos, jewelry, etc. The portion of the card that
recorded alcohol purchases had "VOID" written through it – I was
not yet twenty-one years old.

The in-processing was completed by the issuance of a Geneva
Convention Identification Card that declared I was a member of

---

[1] "Dog tag", because of the resemblance to an actual dog tag, was the
unofficial name for the personal identification tags worn by military
personnel. The tag is primarily used for the identification of dead and
wounded. The wearer's blood type was noted along with his/her religion.
Two identical tags were issued. One was worn on a long chain in the event
the wearer was killed and remained with the body. The second tag was
collected for identification purposes.

[2] A card certifying the bearer's right to purchase rationed goods.

the United States Armed Forces and listed my name, rank, service number, and date of birth. *"What's this for?"* I asked. He replied, *"Keep this card with you at all times. If you should ever become a Prisoner of War, the Geneva Convention directs your captors of the humane treatment they're supposed to take with any captive military."* My immediate thoughts wondered if the enemy could read or comprehend anything written in the English language.

The clerk then told me I'd have to attend a mandatory briefing for all personnel arriving in-country. Also, I would need to have my shot record checked at the dispensary. But first, he said I needed to get my personal protection gear issued. (Finally!) I filled out a requisition form indicating my sizes and then I was sent to a central warehouse on base that issued the gear.

I arrived at the warehouse and found the equipment issue counter. Behind the counter was a wiry Tech Sergeant who had a lit cigarette dangling from his lips that bounced when he talked and dropped ashes with every word. I gave him the requisition form and he left the counter, returning shortly with an armload of items. *"Here ya go, sonny… here's all your John Wayne stuff,"* he said. The items included a pair of jungle boots, two sets of jungle fatigues, flak vest, gas mask, canteen, mess kit, ammo pouch, steel helmet, and a helmet liner.

After I blew cigarette ashes off of my new gear, I tried on the boots, flak vest, and helmet while at the counter. The boots and vest were fine but the headband on the helmet was adjusted wide open – the bottom rim of the helmet rested on my nose. *"Isn't this a bit too low?"* I asked. The sergeant chuckled and said, as he dropped more ashes, *"Sonny, it can't get too low. There'll be times you'll wanna climb inside that helmet, trust me."* I didn't need to hear that.

I surveyed all the gear and noticed a missing item. *"What about a weapon?"* I asked. He looked at me like I was an idiot. He removed his cigarette and retorted, *"This here's a warehouse for christsake, not a damn armory. I don't have any weapons here. What you see on this here counter is all you're gonna get from me."* I signed for the issue and thanked him (for some reason). I hauled my new possessions back to the transit quarters with the helmet covering my eyes and doubted seriously that John Wayne ever looked that stupid.

When I arrived at the transit quarters I was eager to try on my

new fatigues. They were made of lightweight green cotton poplin. The long-sleeved shirt consisted of two slant pockets on the chest and two lower bellows pockets. The pants had two hip pockets, two slash pockets at the hips and two bellows pockets on the thigh. The left thigh bellows pocket also had a "hidden" survival pocket located inside. The pants had a button fly and a drawstring in each pants leg.

The jungle boots had olive drab nylon uppers that extended well above the ankle and black leather soles that covered the toes. The boots were not intended to be waterproof – eyelets near the arch were used to drain the boots. The Panama soles had a thin steel spike protection plate embedded to block punji sticks[1].

I took both fatigue shirts to the on-base Vietnamese tailor shop to have insignias sewn on and also to have both shirts altered to short-sleeves which most all Air Force GIs did. I had two stripes sewn on in anticipation of my promotion. Insignias on jungle fatigues were embroidered using black thread – that made rank less conspicuous[2].

I located the clinic and an enlisted corpsman reviewed my shot record to insure I had all the required Vietnam inoculations[3]. I couldn't imagine that I would need any more shots – I had been a human pincushion prior to leaving Lowery AFB. The corpsman said everything looked okay for now but routinely I'd require additional immunizations while in Vietnam. I hoped I'd never need another GG[4] shot – the amount of serum was determined by body weight and, when shot in my butt, left me nearly paralyzed for several days.

I had just enough time to catch some lunch before my next briefing. The chow hall meal was "Chili-Mac" which was a combination of chili and macaroni – an entrée that would have been far more appealing had the air temperature been about sixty degrees cooler.

---

[1] A punji stick is a sharpened bamboo stake, often coated with human excrement, and planted in a shallow pit to wound and infect the feet.
[2] Enemy snipers usually targeted higher-ranking soldiers first.
[3] The required immunizations were smallpox, typhoid, yellow fever, gamma globulin, typhus, tetanus, cholera, plague, and oral polio.
[4] The gamma globulin or "GG" injections were usually given in an attempt to boost immunity against Hepatitis A.

I had just sat down with my meal tray at a vacant table when a three-striper sergeant sat down across from me. The GI had a dark tropical tan, a stubby beard, mildly offensive body odor, wore muddy boots, and had the unmistakable demeanor of a war veteran. He must have noticed my junior rank because he asked, *"Bet you're a FNG[1]...right?"* I had no idea what that meant but I suspected it had something to do with my limited time in-country. I told him I arrived two days ago and that I was going through my in-processing. *"Yeah...I thought so,"* he replied.

We both ate without speaking until about half way through the meal when he leaned across the table and spoke almost in a whisper, *"A piece of advice... you damn well better look after yourself first... cause sure as hell nobody else will... they'll be too busy saving their own ass."* His unsolicited advice startled me and then he added in a softer voice, *"And another thing...don't get too chummy with anyone here cause... who knows... they might get blown to hell tomorrow and you'll feel like shit ...I know... it happened to me."* Apparently overwhelmed by emotion, he squinted his eyes, dropped his head, and squeezed his fist so tight that he bent the spoon he was holding. He leaned back, regained his composure and abruptly left the table exclaiming the food was crap and that he needed a smoke.

I sat there for the longest time trying to make sense of what just happened. Was his advice worth considering or did he just need to vent his feelings... and if so, why did he pick me? The whole episode was very disturbing.

---

[1] "FNG" was a term used for any new guy. The phrase was preceded by an explicative adjective.

That afternoon, I attended a base-wide mandatory briefing for all newcomers. About two-dozen GIs filed into the cramped and hot briefing room. Some appeared more eager than others to be there. I found a seat close to the podium and had a pen and some paper handy. A Master Sergeant entered the room from a rear doorway and made his way to the podium. He began the briefing by reading from a syllabus in a monotone voice:

"On behalf of the United States Air Force and Nha Trang Airbase, I welcome you to Southeast Asia and to Vietnam. It goes without saying that you'd rather not be here, but the fact is you are, so I suggest you make the most out of your experience.

As a member of the U.S. Armed Forces serving in Vietnam, you have certain entitlements. Among the most important is your legal status. Since you are governed by the Uniform Code of Military Justice, you have diplomatic immunity by special concessions of the government of the Republic of Vietnam. Any local incident involving U.S. military personnel will be reported to the Chief of Military Assistance Advisory Group for appropriate disciplinary action. A word of caution gentlemen – don't test the system!

One of our main goals is for you to leave country the same way you entered it – alive! There are some strict do's and don'ts that you need to know and abide by during your tour." I got my pen ready.

"First and foremost, you need to stay alive and stay well! You do this by reducing your vulnerability of getting killed or injured. During a mortar or rocket attack, if you're not near a bunker... get down and stay down." Not a problem! *"Stay low and protect yourself against shrapnel; don't even think about watching the fireworks show. Stay down until the all-clear signal is sounded."* Okay, what exactly is the all-clear signal? *"Be aware that the Viet Cong have been*

known to intentionally cease their assault as a deception that the engagement has terminated only to resume the attack a short time later in hopes of inflicting additional causalities." A significant bit of information worthy of remembering! *"If the need arises, you will be issued a personal sidearm and ammunition by your unit. This action will take place if a ground assault by the enemy is deemed imminent. This is called a Red Option Two."* How often does that happen?

"While in Southeast Asia, you'll need to have a heightened awareness of some health concerns: sunburn, malaria, venereal disease, and crotch rot." Did he say crotch rot? *"You are now in the tropics and the sun's rays are far more intense than you're accustomed. For some servicemen, this condition can and will inflict a sunburn to exposed skin in less than half the time. A word of warning – if you become incapable of performing your duties due to sunburn, this could lead to an Article Fifteen[1].*

Preventing malaria is simple – take a malaria pill each week... and then deal with the side effects. This is a fair trade-off for preventing the disease. Malaria pills are available every Monday morning at all dining facilities."

Prostitutes harbor venereal disease in their bodies, even in their mouths. If you have unprotected intercourse with a prostitute, you <u>*will*</u> *get a venereal disease. The probability of contacting VD is reduced by using a prophylactic."* I felt like I was back in my high school heath class. *"If you believe you have been exposed, report to sick-call immediately. Contacting VD is not grounds for disciplinary*

---

[1] Article 15 is part of the Uniform Code of Military Justice that deals with non-judicial punishment actions. Enlisted servicemen were constantly threatened with this disciplinary tool.

action…not reporting the disease is." I didn't write down any of that information. What about crotch rot?

"Now some advice about crotch rot. The high humidity in Southeast Asia makes for a favorable growth medium for fungi… especially in the groin area and on the feet – anyplace on the body that stays dark and moist. Crotch rot is an advanced case of jock itch and is characterized by intense burning and irritations on and around the genitals. Keeping yourself clean and dry is imperative in preventing the growth and spread of fungus. Using moisture-absorbing powder whenever possible helps this condition. Crotch rot can run rampant during the monsoon season.

In closing, my advice to you is to make the most out of an undesirable situation. Use common sense throughout your tour and take reasonable precautions to keep yourself safe and healthy. Have a good tour."

As we exited the room, each person was issued two booklets. One was a Vietnam Pocket Guide that contained useful information and provided some history of the area. The second book was a Vietnamese Language primer. Following the meeting, I reviewed my notes from the in-brief. I'd written down four things: 1. Don't test the system; 2. Don't get sunburned; 3. Stay low during attacks; 4. Stay clean and dry. The term "ground assault" lingered in my thoughts.

I was introduced to my immediate supervisor, Tech Sergeant Peter Johns, who was the Non-Commissioned Officer in Charge (NCOIC) of the armament work center. He was of medium build, sported a dark mustache and wore black-rimmed glasses. He seemed pleased at my arrival and explained that my job would be primarily working in the phase docks[1]. This was somewhat of a disappointment because I was expecting to load rockets on the aircraft – performing routine preventive maintenance away from the flightline was not high on my agenda.

Sgt. Johns explained my job would initially be cleaning, overhauling, and maintaining the rocket launchers and racks. I joined three other airmen and one staff sergeant who all worked an average of ten hours a day depending on how many aircraft were in the docks. Sgt. Johns mentioned that when the workload would allow it, each person could possibly have one duty-free day per week and that my off day would be scheduled on Tuesdays. He also added that, to the extent possible, off time would be granted to anyone who wanted to attend church services.

The work center operated in two shifts – the early shift usually performed functional checks of different armament components and dealt with problematic systems. The late shift completed the routine cleaning of rocket launchers – a rocket's exhaust would leave an encrusted residue in the launcher tubes that had to be removed using a circular wire brush attached to a long rod. To complete the task, the launcher's tube was swabbed with lightweight oil.

---

[1] After a prescribed amount of flight hours, each aircraft would routinely cycle through the Phase Docks to be thoroughly inspected for wear, corrosion, or battle damage and repaired as needed.

I was anxious to start my job because I needed to prove to myself that I was capable of doing the work. Until then, I had been exclusively in training status and my talents and abilities were unproven – both to the Air Force and to myself. That was my first real duty assignment and I was eager to demonstrate my worth to the work center – the rejection I experienced at Pleiku had severely bruised my ego. However, Sgt. Johns knew nothing about that episode so I really was making a fresh start. I could hardly wait to start working!

Chapter 7

"The Most Alluring Amenity"

Nha Trang

"I know God will not give me anything I can't handle. I just wish that He didn't trust me so much."
Mother Teresa

Set on the eastern seaboard of the Indochinese Peninsula, Nha Trang is located at 12 degrees north latitude[1] in the Ngoc Hoi river delta that forms a level coastal plain in the shadow of the Truong  Son mountain range. Nha Trang is endowed with deep, quiet, and warm waters surrounded by archipelagoes, mountains, and nearly four miles of white silica sand beach. Nha Trang is sunny all year, except for the monsoon season, which typically spans September through December. The average temperature is 74°F with the hottest months being June, July, and August.

One legend of Nha Trang's name origin comes from the Vietnamese pronunciation of a Cham word "Eatran" that can be loosely translated as "Reed River." According to the legend, there once was an abundant amount of reeds along the Ngoc Hoi River.

---

[1] Nha Trang is 840 miles above the equator.

The river flows past the ancient Cham temple and empties into the South China Sea.

Nha Trang is the capitol of the Khánh Hòa Province, a 2,014 square mile region in the South Central Coast. Vietnam is divided into 59 provinces (known in Vietnamese as tinh). The provinces are further subdivided into districts, provincial cities, and towns.

Without a doubt, the most alluring amenity about Nha Trang was its famous beach – miles of white sand shaped in a picturesque

sweeping crescent. Typical to most tropical locations, the turquoise water was warm and nearly transparent with an array of marine life. A section of the beach near the entrance of the airbase was set aside for members of the U.S. Armed Forces and was readily accessible under normal security conditions. On occasion the ocean was off limits due to jellyfish or shark sightings.

Nha Trang Airbase was positioned next to the shoreline and was home to about 3,000 servicemen[1]. The French built the base in 1949, and it was known as "Base Aerienne 194." At sixteen feet above sea level,

---

[1]   I did not encounter any female GIs during my time there even though 7,484 women served in the military in Vietnam (8 were killed).

the main asphalt runway was 6,166-feet long and could accommodate most cargo aircraft except the larger and heavier aircraft that required a concrete runway. Most all of the aircraft on the flightline were parked in protective fortifications called revetments – high double-walled steel partitions filled with stone riprap that would protect aircraft from mortar and rocket attacks.

The major military unit at Nha Trang Airbase was the 14th Air Commando Wing, the only outfit of its kind in the U. S. Air Force. Squadrons within the Wing were deployed throughout the theater and provided close-in ground support with their AC-47 gunships[1].

The 21st Tactical Air Support Squadron (21st TASS) was a tenant organization of the airbase and its primary mission was to provide air reconnaissance and direct air strikes for fighter aircraft. This was accomplished with some of the smallest aircraft in the Air Force inventory. One particular aircraft was called a "Bird Dog" because it would spot a target like a pointer dog would spot game fowl.

Pilots of these air reconnaissance aircraft were referred to as Forward Air Controllers – or better known as "FACs." These often neglected pilots lacked the prestige of flying high-tech fighter jets, but their role was dignified by the enormous risks they took to coordinate air attacks. The rules of engagement in South Vietnam required a FAC to direct all air strikes to ensure fighter pilots put

---

[1] My original orders had me assigned to one of these squadrons at Pleiku.

their ordnance on target and to lessen the risk of hitting allied forces or civilians.

A good FAC needed a fighter pilot's frame of mind but was obliged to operate at the slow pace of a World War I bi-plane. If a ground target was identified, the FAC would mark the target area with smoke rockets and radio the loitering "fast-movers" to initiate an air assault using its smoke as a reference point. Following the attack, the FAC would return to the area for a damage assessment, body count and, if necessary (or possible), call in another strike.

FACs usually conducted surveillance in the same geographical area. By becoming familiar with the landscape, they were better able to detect subtle changes that might indicate enemy activity.

Another risky tactic for FACs was "trolling" – flying low and slow to serve as bait hoping to draw ground fire, thus revealing the enemy's position. FACs would jokingly describe the engagement in this manner, *"We flew around until we got shot at, and then called in an air strike."*

The only Medal of Honor bestowed to a FAC was posthumously awarded to 33 year-old Captain Hillard Wilbanks, a member of the 21st TASS, for sacrificing his life on February 24, 1967. Captain Wilbanks held off a sizable Viet Cong force from ambushing a battalion of South Vietnamese Army Rangers by firing his M-16 out the window of his Bird Dog. He was mortally wounded and his aircraft was lost. He was within two months of returning home to his wife and four small children.

The 21st TASS Commander at the time of my arrival was Lt. Col. Karl T. Feuerriegel, who had been the CO[1] since the previous March. He was awarded the prestigious Air Force Cross[2] for extraordinary heroism during the Tết Offensive in January 1968. Col. Feuerriegel was a likeable middle-aged aviator who saw extensive action in World War II as a B-24 bomber pilot with the Army Air Corps. As a squadron commander, his leadership style was laid back – until you really screwed up and then you got a taste of his wrath.

The 21st TASS flew two different aircraft – the O1E/F *"Bird Dog"* (a militarized Cessna 172 equipped with an oversized engine[3]), and the O-2A *"Skymaster"* (military version of the Cessna 337). In both cases, the "O" prefix indicated an observation aircraft. The O-1 Bird Dog carried four rockets under each wing, lacked any armor protection[4] and did not have self-sealing fuel tanks – ground fire hitting the wings often resulted in a crash landing due to fuel starvation. Also, because of its conventional landing gear, the O-1 was notorious for ground looping – an occurrence that is characterized by the aircraft's tail suddenly (and sometimes violently) swinging around, usually during breaking after a landing[5].

---

[1] Commanding Officer

[2] The citation read in part, *"Despite great personal risk from heavy automatic weapons fire, Lt. Col. Karl T. Feuerriegel repeatedly attacked hostile positions in an O-2 aircraft armed with high explosive rockets. He systematically silenced three machine gun positions and neutralized two fortified hostile companies, thereby preventing the annihilation of beleaguered friendly units."*

[3] Equipped with a 213 hp Continental flat six-piston engine, the Bird Dog was easily capable of aerobatics, but such maneuvers were explicitly prohibited.

[4] Some FAC pilots chose to sit on their flak vest instead of wearing it because ground fire usually penetrated the fuselage from underneath the aircraft.

[5] In 1966, more O-1s were lost to accidents than to enemy action primarily due to pilots having limited or no experience in such a light aircraft with a conventional landing gear.

The O-2A *Skymaster* was originally destined to replace the older O-1 aircraft because it was faster, more maneuverable, and offered better protection to pilots. The *Skymaster* could carry twenty-eight rockets in four pods, two under each wing. The O-2A forward

engine propeller operated in undisturbed air while the rear engine sliced through turbulent air coming off the airframe. In concert, the two engines produced a very unique characteristic sound that was unmistakable and often provoked fear in enemy forces.

The squadron was located adjacent to the flightline toward the end and southwest side of Runway 30. The administrative offices were housed in a two-story building with the phase docks in a yard area on the east side. Probably the most popular spot at the squadron was the mailroom located on the second floor of the administration building. In-coming mail was sorted alphabetically according to servicemen's last names and a clerk would hand GIs their letters through a mail window.

The flightline was located between the squadron area and the runway. Three rows of revetments provided parking and tie-down for the squadron's aircraft. A large barrel of water was placed near each aircraft to extinguish any leaky white phosphorous[1] rocket warheads.

The Armament work center occupied a portion of a large metal building along with the Radio/Comm, Supply, Electrical, and

---

[1] White phosphorous will self-ignite when exposed to the air and liquefy at 111 degrees F.

Instrument work centers. The temperature inside the building was significantly higher than the outside ambient air and a single floor fan ran continuously but offered little relief. Because of this sweltering working condition, we were allowed to remove our fatigue shirts while on duty.

In all, the 21st TASS community was a fairly close-knit unit with most everyone willing to go a second mile for the good of the squadron. Whenever causalities occurred within the unit, everyone grievously felt it[1].

---

[1]   The 21st TASS had a total of 20 causalities – 17 officers and 3 enlisted men.

Chapter 8

"Flightline Hilton"

June – August 1968

> *"The optimist sees opportunity in every danger;*
> *the pessimist sees danger in every opportunity."*
> Winston Churchill

In the News...

* *Senator Robert Kennedy was fatally wounded in a Los Angeles hotel after giving a victory speech to celebrate his win in the California Primary. The 42-year-old Senator was greeting hotel workers while being escorted through the pantry of the Ambassador Hotel when a Palestinian immigrant named Sirhan Sirhan, fired shots from a .22 caliber handgun.*

* *The Democratic National Convention was held in Chicago to select their nominee for President. Their selection process was particularly difficult due to a split in the party over the Vietnam War. On one side, Eugene McCarthy put forward a decidedly anti-war campaign, calling for the immediate withdrawal from the region. On the other side, Hubert H. Humphrey called for a policy more in line with President Johnson's, which focused on making any reduction of force contingent on concessions extracted from the Paris Peace Talks. Anti-war demonstrators protested throughout the convention, clashing with police all around the convention center. The Democrats eventually settled on Humphrey.*

* *The United States and North Vietnam agreed on Paris, France as the site for preliminary peace talks. Meanwhile in Saigon, communist forces launched a major ground attack using both mortars and rockets. This offense was coordinated with attacks at other major cities of South Vietnam including Nha Trang.*

* *In July, Gen. Creighton Abrams replaced Gen. William Westmoreland as the U.S. Commander in South Vietnam.*

* *The U.S. Command in Saigon reported the U.S combat deaths in Vietnam had risen to more than 25,000. The death toll in the first seven months of 1968 exceeded that of all 12 months of 1967.*

* *Typhoon Shirley made a direct hit on Hong Kong in late August with 110-knot winds. The storm began as a depression in the western Pacific near Manila, and tracked eastward toward the South China Sea with an expected landfall somewhere in Vietnam. However, the storm made a northwesterly turn and headed straight for Hong Kong.*

* *The U.S. fiscal year ended on June 30 with a deficit of $25.4 billion. Meanwhile, President Johnson asked Congress for a supplemental $3.9 billion for the Vietnam conflict.*

This time period was one of becoming accustomed to my new surroundings and getting acclimated to a new way of life. This was also a time of discovery, because everything I experienced and witnessed was a new occurrence. I was like a dry sponge – soaking everything up and trying desperately to make sense of it all. The H&I fire became more of an assurance than an annoyance and the nightly flares offered comfort. This being my first real duty assignment, I had to get used to working with people who were higher in rank – especially officers.

My body eventually acclimated to being in the tropics, but not until after my digestive system went through a few predictable cycles of nausea and diarrhea. The incessant heat became tolerable because there was no air conditioning to offer contrast. I suffered from head colds for the first few months, which most likely were allergies from the flora in Southeast Asia.

My first letter from Barbara arrived in early June – it had been eleven days[1] since I first wrote her. Her 16-page letter was written over several days and was mailed to me when she learned my address. The mail clerk was delighted when my letter arrived because I had loitered by the pickup window every day at mail call hoping for a letter.

I must have read her letter at least a dozen times – each time in seclusion to conceal my emotions. I could almost hear her voice as I read the words. It was incredibly comforting having that far-away connection with my bride. All of her letters became a treasure for me, and I became very protective of each one of them.

I attempted to write her every day and sometimes it was just a short one-paragraph letter saying good night[2]. My intent was to assure her of my well being on a daily basis. When time allowed, I wrote longer letters describing my new lifestyle and sharing my thoughts on various topics. I was careful not to include all the details, as I did in my first letter, in fear that some would be too disturbing. Letters mailed from Vietnam were free of charge – the word *"Free"* was handwritten on the envelope where a stamp would have been. Barbara didn't have that privilege… her airmail stamp cost a dime.

✶✶✶✶✶

At long last, all the paperwork and routine in-processing were completed and I began reporting for duty at the armament work center. I was assigned a trainer whom I shadowed for a while in order to learn the ropes. I discovered the nature of the work on the

---

[1] The one-way delivery time to and from Vietnam was typically five days.

[2] My daily letters to Barbara became my primary source of information for this manuscript.

late shift required hardly any proficiency in the discipline – the tasks were repetitive in nature and once I learned the routine, it was almost robotic.

The early shift was far more appealing because we dealt with problematic systems rather than routine tasks. Whenever an electrical problem was encountered, it presented me a challenge and a welcomed opportunity to keep my skills honed. I was also surprised to discover the daily routine would be so similar to that of a stateside job – I reported to the work center, did my job, and then went "home" to the barracks. I didn't have set working hours per se, but the time on the job was somewhat predictable.

I came to realize this mundane assignment wasn't all that bad when compared to most GIs' primary roles in Vietnam – most would gladly trade places with me in a heartbeat. It took constant effort to keep things in proper perspective.

*****

I was anticipating two events that were late in coming – my promotion to Airman First Class (E-3) and my relocation to permanent quarters. June arrived with no promotion orders. I thought maybe the official notification was sent to the 4th ACS at Pleiku but was tossed away because I wasn't assigned there. Sgt. Johns told me to be patient because, *"Things move a lot slower in Southeast Asia."* That offered little consolation.

My promotion wasn't a matter of money as much as a way to conceal my in-country newness. I was getting paranoid with the single "mosquito-wing" stripe on my uniform. I desperately wanted to blend into the ranks of the veteran workforce, but my boyish face – barely past the peach fuzz stage – easily defied that persona.

Regardless, two stripes on my uniform would help a little. As for the move out of the transit barracks, a vacancy in the squadron's cantonment area simply didn't exist. *"Maybe sometime this month,"* was the typical answer to my repetitive question, *"When?"*

✶✶✶✶✶

The airbase used a system of alert levels to indicate the current defense posture. The most common, and least threatening, was "Code White." No restrictions were placed on routine activities and the base operated under normal conditions. Under a "Code Gray," awareness was increased and activities were limited to official business only. When enemy activity was anticipated, but no engagement had occurred, the level was elevated to "Yellow Alert." During this alert, vigilance was maximized and a mass assembly of servicemen was not allowed – like at the nightly movie, church, or on the beach.

The highest level of security was a "Red Alert" and it could be an Option I or Option II, the former being an air assault, i.e. bombs, mortars or rockets, and the latter being a ground assault indicating an attack by ground forces.

The base routinely practiced for a Red Option II by issuing

sidearms to every serviceman. M-16 rifles were stored in large walk-in metal buildings called a Conex that were strategically located through-out the base. During the practice, we were required to be in battle gear and file past the squadron's Conex to retrieve our rifle.

It puzzled me that we were never issued ammunition, but hoped surely that during an actual Red Option II, they'd hand out ammunition clips with the rifles. On second thought, maybe it was best that we didn't have bullets during a practice alert – there's a fair chance we'd self-inflict more casualties than the enemy could ever achieve.

The practice alert never lasted more than two hours, and when it terminated, we would clear our weapon with the rifle's muzzle aimed into a red metal drum filled with sand – just in case a round had somehow made it into the breech. If the weapon did discharge, the sand would safely absorb the projectile.

★★★★★

June 4th marked our one-month wedding anniversary and my memory still held vivid images of our wedding and honeymoon. But such memories were like a different era and now I was in another. I couldn't determine which was more surreal – my being married or being in Vietnam.

I couldn't believe how quickly the month had passed. I was told that my year in Vietnam would be the quickest one of my life. I sure hoped so because I had a lot of time to consume before my DEROS and just thinking about it in terms of days was so overwhelming.

Some GIs endured the self-imposed drudgery of marking off each day on a calendar, which made their tour seem like an eternity. I avoided that trap by beginning each morning, not with an "X" on the calendar, but with an attitude to combat any negative aspects toward anything that might happen that day. Such a stance served me well and made the time pass quickly.

*****

One of my first items to be issued at the work center was a personal toolbox. That shouldn't have surprised me because my career classification was a weapons *mechanic*. Each person in the work center had an identical toolbox and we were held accountable for its contents. A routine tool inventory was mandatory after any maintenance activity to ensure we didn't accidentally leave a screwdriver, a set of pliers, or any other tool pigeonholed in an aircraft. Any foreign object, especially a tool, could possibly jam the flight controls and have disastrous consequences.

When two or more people were working in close quarters, it wasn't uncommon for tools to get shuffled, and that created a shortage or overage during an inventory. One afternoon during an infrequent lull period, I laid out all of my tools on a cloth on the floor and applied a light mist of green spray paint to help identify my tools from those belonging to others. The staff sergeant in our shop thought that was a brilliant idea so he sprayed his tools in a similar manner. The imbecile used the same color paint!

*****

Meals for GIs ranked E-5 and below were served in a new 200-seat dining hall, but it was better known as the "chow hall." Senior NCOs[1] and officers usually had meals at their respective dining facilities. Despite the fact that hardly anything was fresh except the bread, the chow hall food was surprisingly appetizing. The milk and

---

[1] Non-Commissioned Officer

eggs were from dehydrated powder and the rest of the food was canned goods.

The dining hall employed Vietnamese as kitchen helpers,  dishwashers, and janitors. These employees, who were mostly female, were entitled to dining privileges. This was readily obvious by their appearance – they were plump almost to the point of obesity. It was odd seeing a portly Vietnamese – most were lean and slender. I wonder how many years we shortened their lives with our western diet, laden with fat and calories.

Bread was baked daily and was always delicious. On one occasion, the flour used for the bread became infested with small beetle grubs that were too numerous to remove, so the bread was baked still impregnated with these bugs. As expected, complaints soared from the GIs about these "crispy critters."

The Mess Sergeant did a brilliant thing – he threw a handful of raisins into each batch of bread dough and announced that all bread served in his chow hall would now be *raisin* bread. Afterwards, when a patron discovered a dark speck in his bread, he assumed (or pretended) it was a raisin and the gripes soon ended.

✶✶✶✶✶

While in the chow hall one morning in early June, I noticed the headline on the *Pacific Stars and Stripes* newspaper being read by a serviceman sitting at a nearby table. The headline read *"Kennedy Slain."* That's odd... President Kennedy had been dead for almost five years. Maybe it was an old newspaper – but it looked too new to be five years old. I asked the GI and he said, *"Not JFK... it's his brother Robert. Somebody wasted him in LA yesterday."*

I was troubled by that news... not that I was a Kennedy supporter, but because of yet another vicious assassination of a prominent leader in our country. The decade already had its fair share of unrest and turmoil – two months previously, Martin Luther King Jr. had been gunned down in Memphis.

The root of the tumult was attributed, in no small part, to Civil Rights issues and to the increasing objection to our involvement in the Vietnam War which was in a quagmire with no apparent means of escape. Civil unrest abounded and the conditions were volatile with riots breaking out all across the country. In some strange way, I felt safer in Vietnam than in the streets back home.

★★★★★

When an aircraft was released from the phase docks, it had to undergo a Functional Check Flight (FCF) to thoroughly verify that every system was operating properly before it was returned to service. Squadron pilots, whose sole job was to test-flight the aircraft, conducted the FCFs.

In mid June, I cleared a write-up on an O-1E Bird Dog that involved re-soldering a wire on the #3 rocket launcher. When Captain Richardson, the FCF pilot, reviewed the aircraft log, he wanted to speak with the person who did the repair. The officer asked me, *"Are you absolutely certain this bird will fire a rocket from number three launcher? This is a repeat write-up and I wanna make damn sure it's fixed this time!"*

I swallowed hard and replied in my most confident voice, *"Yes sir, this aircraft is fully capable of firing rockets from all launchers."* In reality, I wasn't certain at all that my repair job had fixed the problem... but I had to say something to make him believe the issue had been resolved, even at the risk of damaging my credibility and personal integrity. After I quickly replied to the Captain, I realized what a dumb response that was!

The captain looked me straight in the eye and said, *"Well, I hope it's fixed...for your sake. Check out a headset, you're going with me."* What? He wanted me to fly in the Bird Dog...and fire rockets? Surely not...so I had to ask, *"Sir, you want me on the FCF to test fire the launcher?"* The pilot answered sarcastically, *"Well now, I can't fire rockets from the aircraft while it is still on the ground, now can I?"* I answered, *"No sir, I suppose not."* Then he added, *"Be ready to go in twenty minutes...and make sure you have dog tags[1]."*

I felt that I'd just jumped out of the frying pan into the fire. Did Captain Richardson want to put me on the spot by insisting that I personally observe that the aircraft still had a problem? I was in a quandary so I approached Sgt. Johns and asked for his advice. He asked, *"You were confident enough to sign off the write-up so why do you think the aircraft might still have a problem?"* He had a valid point – I had done all that I could to verify a working system so my comment to the FCF pilot was justified. Sgt. Johns also said he had flown on several FCFs and that I would benefit from the experience.

I got to the aircraft early and loaded four rockets under each wing. Captain Richardson arrived and performed a thorough pre-

---

[1] Dog tags were required for all aircrew to assist in positive identification of the body in case of a fatal crash.

flight inspection of the Bird Dog. I climbed into the rear seat directly behind the pilot's seat and buckled my shoulder and lap belts. The rear or "observer's" seat had a control stick, rudder pedals, and an engine mixture and throttle control – I was very careful not to touch them. I thought all aircrews had to undergo indoctrination, survival training, or something before being allowed to ride backseat in a Bird Dog. I was wrong.

We taxied to the runway and received our take-off clearance from the control tower. The pilot pushed the throttle forward and the engine responded with a roar. The aircraft began to roll forward  and as we quickly picked up speed, the aircraft's tail raised parallel to the runway. He then pulled back on the control stick and we became airborne... almost like we were floating. The ride was a bit bumpy and very noisy – the side windows were open and the wind noise was loud...but the breeze felt wonderful.

We flew northwest through a valley and passed over numerous rice patties to an open grassland area. There the pilot called someone over the radio named *"Ragged Scooper*[1]*"* and requested permission to fire rockets. After a short while, a voice over the radio reported no known friendly forces or Victor Charlie in the sector and gave consent for the rocket fire.

---

[1] *Ragged Scooper"* was the call sign for the Direct Air Support Center (DASC). What made that call sign unique was that it was awkward for Americans to say...and almost impossible for the Vietnamese that might be trying to intercept our frequency.

Captain Richardson asked me over the intercom if I was ready. *"Yes sir,"* I replied as I pulled my lap and shoulder belts a little tighter. The pilot reached up over his head to the armament panel and energized the system with the Master Arm switch. He gained altitude and pulled the nose high – almost in a stall – then made an abrupt wingover to the left that turned instantly into a near vertical dive. Now headed toward the ground at a sharp angle, the aircraft quickly gained speed. My gut started to quiver – like a feeling caused by the first plunge of a roller coaster...only far more intense. Captain Richardson selected the #3 launcher – the final action to fire the rocket was to pull the trigger on the control stick. *"Please...oh please let it work!"* I frantically thought to myself. We continued downward for what seemed like an eternity. I became really concerned and thought, *"It didn't fire...the rocket didn't fire!"*

No sooner than that thought passed my mind, I heard a very loud *SWOOOSH* as the #3 rocket came to life under the left wing

and departed the launcher with a fiery exhaust. The rocket fins folded out just beyond the aircraft and the warhead self-armed. The rocket raced ahead of the Bird Dog until it hit the ground and detonated creating a massive cloud of white smoke. The pilot pulled out of the dive and the G-force crunched me into the seat.

Wow...what a ride! One moment I was nearly weightless and then the next, I experienced the gravity force of twice my weight! As we regained altitude I looked back over my shoulder and saw the huge smoke cloud lingering at the point of impact. I had never experienced anything like that...*it was totally awesome!*

I was incredibly relieved that the launcher had fired! My heart was still racing when he said, *"Well, looks like it's fixed this time...good work Airman."* Was that a compliment? *"Thank you sir...will you be firing the remaining rockets?"* I really wanted to do that again. *"No, the other launchers are okay...it was only number three that needed to be test fired."* We flew straight back to the airbase and landed. The return trip to base was much different, in terms of my anxiety, than the trip out to fire the rocket.

Not just anyone would ever have the opportunity to do what I had just done...especially a "mosquito wing" Airman. I felt somewhat privileged – like I had gained entry into some exclusive fraternity. It gave me a new perspective of the importance of my job. Maybe that's the real reason the FCF pilot wanted me to fly backseat. I'm glad my dog tags weren't needed.

✶✶✶✶✶

For a while I was assigned late duty, which freed up my morning hours. The incessant heat from the morning sun cut short any attempt for any additional sack-time. I wanted to visit the beach, but the idea of leaving a secure airbase seemed a bit foolish. I occupied my off-duty time by reading and other passive pursuits ... all the while, the lure of a tropical beach was ever present.

With ample encouragement from fellow servicemen, I eventually attained sufficient nerve to venture beyond the confines of the airbase. I altered an old pair of fatigue trousers into a swimsuit – not in my wildest dreams did I ever think I'd need a swimsuit in Vietnam! I boarded a military bus that made routine runs into town, and the first stop was the beach located just outside the main gate of the airbase.

When I stepped off the bus, a gentle sea breeze greeted me but the radiant heat from the sun-baked sand was almost overbearing. The beach was nicer than I'd imagined and the scene could have easily been on a post card. The crescent shoreline had a wide stretch of white sand with palm trees along the nearby roadway. The essence of that strikingly beautiful and serene scene was in sharp contrast to the cruelties of a war happening nearby.

The beach was occupied with about two-dozen servicemen – some in the water, some lying on mats in the sun, but most in the shade of the several thatched-roof canopies that lined the upper part of the beach. I chose an unoccupied canopy and was grateful for the shade – it was nearing the middle of the day when the sun's rays were most intense, and June was one of the hottest months of the year.

Near the roadway I saw something I couldn't believe – a  miniature putt-putt golf course right there on the beach! I later discovered this popular attraction was constructed from surplus building material by a Red Horse Civil Engineering unit[1].

---

[1] The VC had targeted the golf course twice during recent mortar attacks – most likely with the idea it would have a demoralizing effect. Each time however, the facility was quickly rebuilt.

The South China Sea was surprisingly calm with hardly any wave action. Several small islands dotted the seascape, which I surmised was a submerged mountain range with its tops protruding above sea level. The largest and closest was Hon Tre Island where several U.S. military units were located, including the Army 5th Special Forces Detachment that operated a POW detention unit on the island.

As I gazed out at the tranquil ocean, I became awestruck by all that I was seeing – the reality of the moment was mind-boggling. I visualized "home" being just beyond the ocean horizon but totally out of reach… I felt as if I was being held captive in that foreign land – so close but yet so far away. GIs constantly referred to the United States as *"The World"* implying Vietnam was not an occupant of the planet.

The mid-morning heat became intense and I decided to cool off with a dip in the ocean. I slipped off my shirt and flip-flops and began walking toward the water. After about ten steps, I quickly realized how incredibly dumb that was – the blistering sand was scorching my feet! I began to hop on one foot and then the other trying to keep both feet in the air as much as possible. I must have looked ridiculous because I heard chuckles from some of the other GIs nearby. When I made it back to my canopy and plopped down to rub my burning feet, one of the other servicemen asked, *"New guy, right?"* I felt pretty stupid and replied, *"Yeah, does it show that bad?"* He said, *"Like a preacher in a whorehouse."*

I did take a swim, the second time wearing shoes to the water's edge. The water was warm, clear, very therapeutic, and I enjoyed it immensely. Being raised in Atlanta, I seldom had the opportunity to be near or swim in the ocean, and I was amazed at how buoyant

I was in salt water. I made a mental note to mention in my next letter to Barbara that I could use a real swimsuit. I felt certain she would consider that a bizarre request.

It was getting near time to leave so I packed up and waited beside the road for the bus (which was running late). Once back on base I took a cold shower to wash off the salty sea water and noticed right away a burning sensation on the back of my neck. Despite the warnings, I got sunburned in that short amount of time. Again, I thought to myself, *"Welcome to Vietnam!"*

★★★★★

The Base Chapel was located near the center of the airbase and had an eighty-seat sanctuary that served Protestant, Catholic, Latter Day Saints, and Christian Science faiths. The Chapel offered daily devotions each morning and three Protestant worship services on Sunday. Adjacent to the sanctuary, and connect-ed by a breezeway, were the Chaplains' offices.

On June 9, 1968 I attended my first worship service. It was a Communion Service and I was surprised to see so few people there – I couldn't imagine not paying homage to God especially while in a war zone. Sadly, I later found out that the sparse attendance was typical. The following congregational prayer was read aloud by everyone:

"O Lord, we have been called to be in this place at this time. May we be mindful of the responsibilities which are ours as military personnel — to maintain order, to establish a rule of law, to protect the peace. Make us obedient always to the laws of God. Grant that in the hour of temptation we may exercise self-control and not be guilty of living an immoral life. Help us to use our skills for strengthening of the nation. Give us faith in God, and help us to demonstrate our faith by regular worship of Thee in the chapel and in our own private world. Through Jesus Christ our Lord. Amen"

I couldn't help but notice a very nice Hammond[1] organ in the sanctuary. This really sparked my interest because music had been a

big part of my life — I started music lessons on the accordion at age seven and my parents bought an organ when I was thirteen. The two years prior to my enlistment, I had played dinner music on an organ at a local restaurant in West Atlanta. I sorely missed my music and longed for the opportunity to play again.

After the service, I spoke with Capt. William S. Schuermann, the Protestant Chaplain, about playing the organ. He was delighted at my request because the current organist was leaving soon and they didn't have a replacement. He said the organist was paid $100 per month and wanted to know when I could begin. Unfortunately,

---

[1] Hammond is the brand name of a popular electric organ. The organ was a gift from a charitable organization somewhere in Ohio. It had been slightly damaged by a mortar attack but still worked well.

I seldom played religious music – most all my repertoire was dinner music and secular in nature.

I respectfully declined his offer but still asked permission to play. Capt. Schuermann said he enjoyed popular music but the other Chaplain detested anything but sacred melodies. He advised me to come by on Tuesdays (the other Chaplain's day off) and I could play any type of music for as long as I desired. That worked well for me because I was off-duty on most Tuesdays.

Playing the organ again was so enjoyable and therapeutic – it was a great substitute for aspirin. I must have played for at least two hours during my first session. It was strange to hear popular tunes being played in a church environment, but nobody seemed to mind. The Chaplain once again encouraged me to reconsider the offer. Again, I respectfully declined. In my next letter to my parents, I asked them to send me some of my secular sheet music.

*****

As I became more at ease with my new surroundings, I became more philosophical in my thinking. I began to contemplate the rationale of war – something I had never done before. I still was ignorant as to why we were fighting, but I sensed the underlying principles of war were against everything that I knew and understood as being right. I felt a disturbing tug-of-war between my involvement in the war effort and my personal moral ethics.

After eighteen days in country, and the first day I attended a worship service, I wrote the following letter to my bride whom I missed dreadfully:

Sunday night
June 9. 1968
11:35 PM

Dear Sweetheart,

Hi again Darling. I couldn't get off to sleep for some reason. That's strange because I was tired. Maybe I'm tensed up – I don't know. I do know that I love you more than anyone knows. Barbara, I miss you so much and need you.

I've been thinking tonight and a little crying too I admit. Sometimes I wish that there were no such thing as a memory. At times like this, a memory can do more harm than good because it makes me miss you twice as much and makes me so lonesome. I'll be so happy when I can come back to you where I belong. I love you, my Darling.

Honey, the moon is so beautiful tonight. It's full and brings back great memories. I'm outside of the barracks in the cooler night air. It's such a beautiful night – all of the stars are out and twinkling – the big moon and the warm glow it's putting out – just to think there's a war going on under such a lovely sky. Why can't people be friends and love thy neighbor?

Honey, excuse me if I'm talking too serious. Once in a while I've got to express my inner thoughts – just like now – all that quietness and beauty was broken by a heavy artillery cannon blasting away, reminding everyone to kill. It's really a shame – wars are useless, they don't prove a thing, and they're so costly – in more ways than one. Wars cause sadness and grief – all so very unnecessary.

I love you, Barbara and I'm very sorry our marriage had to begin in this way. It's so hard on both of us. Well, I figure my kiss should be just west of Hawaii by now. It's coming to you just like I will real soon now. I'd guess I'd better get back in the barracks and try to get to sleep. 6:30 AM will come quick as it is. I feel much better now Dear, thanks for the listen.

I'll say goodnight again.

Love, Dean

★★★★★

A vacancy finally opened in the squadron's barracks, and I was next on the list. Thirty barracks, housing GIs from several different squadrons, were in a cantonment area directly across the road from our squadron. The French built them during their occupation in Vietnam during the 1950's. Each barracks housed eighteen servicemen and was a single-story wooden structure built on a concrete slab with  terracotta style gable roof. Large screened windows afforded cross ventilation, and each window had a wooden shutter hinged at the top that could be lowered by a rope from inside the building. Nine bunk beds and eighteen metal lockers were in each barracks. A small degree of privacy was achieved by the placement of the lockers to create small cubicles. Two GIs shared each cubicle and were considered "roommates." The barracks had electricity[1] that powered two overhead paddle fans, lights, electrical outlets, and an old refrigerator in a small space at the rear of the barracks called a "Day Room."

Perhaps the most distinguishing addition to each barracks was a permanent bunker that surrounded the outside perimeter. The bunker was basically a four-foot high wall created by two sheets of plywood spaced eighteen inches apart – much like a form for a concrete wall except filled with sand. The sand would hopefully absorb shrapnel from any exploding rocket or mortar, shielding the

---

[1] Electricity was produced on base by several massive engine generators.

occupants if they were below the level of the bunker. Of course, if the barracks took a direct hit from above, the perimeter bunker would be useless. My first observation was that the top berth of every bunk bed was well above the level of the bunker. I wondered if that fact bothered anyone else besides me.

Just outside the rear entrance of the barracks was a "community" bunker that could hold about forty people. This was a preferred bunker because it was covered and provided protection from above – the

only trouble was having enough time to get to it. We seldom had any pre-warning of an attack… so I was told.

I moved into barracks 1416 which was duped *"Flightline Hilton"* and was assigned the top bunk (where else?). Everyone said top bunks were cooler because you're at window level and can enjoy an infrequent breeze. My bunk had mosquito netting that hampered any breeze whatsoever.

My roommate was Richard Bush from somewhere in upstate New York. He worked in the avionics work center as a communications technician – the very career field for which I had hoped! Richard had a March DEROS and would separate from the Air Force when he rotated home. The "barracks chief" was usually the highest-ranking person in the barracks, and in our case, he was a Tech Sergeant who was overly paranoid with the water level in the bottle of the water dispenser. If the level became less than three-quarters full, he'd demand that it be filled to the top – usually by the lowest ranking person in the barracks... and that would be me. All water on base was potable but sometimes had a chemical taste due to the purification process. *Kool Aid* drink mix was very popular to mask the taste of the water. A restriction on water usage was sometimes enforced but not on a regular basis.

★★★★★

Vietnamese women were employed at each barracks as housemaids – more commonly known as a *"mamasan."* These older women lived near Nha Trang and commuted to and from the airbase each day. Mamasans were looked upon as transparent fixtures in the barracks and most GIs exhibited little to no modesty in their presence – the gender difference was totally disregarded. GIs communicated with the mamasans mostly with gestures and other non-verbal means. Most mamasans knew a few English words and some GIs learned a few Vietnamese phrases – most of which were vulgar.

The mamasan assigned to my barracks was named Bá Klaum[1]. She stood no more than five feet tall and had a slender build with

---

[1] The prefix Bá refers to a married women much like "Mrs."

small almond shaped eyes. She looked to be in her mid-thirties but her age was deceiving because the typical life span of a Vietnamese seldom surpassed the age of fifty.

Her shoulder-length black hair was usually pulled back into a bun and she normally wore a loose baggy blouse, dark silken slacks, and sandals that flapped against the concrete floor when she walked. Occasionally she would wear traditional Vietnamese apparel called an Áo dài – a long-sleeved blouse with a high collar and a long tunic that was slit on the sides and worn over loose slacks. When outside, she shaded the hot sun with a conical straw hat that tied under her chin with scarf-like material.

She was an incredibly hard worker – her daily routine included making bunks, sweeping the floor, shining boots, and doing

laundry. Every day she would empty each GI's laundry bag, hand-wash each article of clothing, dry the clothes in the sun, iron and fold the clothes, and return them at the end of each day to the foot of each bunk. Since I was a newcomer to the barracks, Bá Klaum collected every article of clothing I owned and marked each item with a unique symbol that identified me from everyone else. This allowed her to return clothing to its proper owner after the daily washings. Barbara jokingly suggested I bring Bá Klaum home as our housekeeper.

For all this service, each serviceman paid her 750 Piaster[1] per month. With eighteen GIs in the barracks, this totaled 13,500 Piaster (or $114.41) which was a respectful income for a Vietnamese woman. Being a mamasan at the airbase was looked upon in high regard and this type of employment was very prestigious and competitive.

Something that really bothered me was how disrespectful many servicemen were toward the mamasans. Some GIs would often take advantage of the language barrier and verbally abuse the women. The men would smile while they were cursing the women – the mamasans would smile back while nodding their heads, not realizing they were being slandered.  Some guys even made a sick game of it. My upbringing wouldn't allow me to tolerate such disrespect – but I was in no position to stop it... yet.

---

[1] 750 Piaster was Vietnamese currency worth about $6.35 in U.S. dollars.

★★★★★

Whenever security conditions were favorable, nightly semi-current Hollywood movies were shown at an outdoor area called the *Dustbowl Theater* – a fairly large assembly arena across the road from the chow hall. Rows of wooden benches faced a large white movie screen and a metal canopy covered the entire area[1].

Before the showing of the nightly movie, the projectionist was obligated to make the following announcement: *"In the event of an*

attack during tonight's movie, do not panic. Take cover on the ground immediately and stay there. All non-essential personnel should remain in the area until the all-clear signal is given." The movie patrons, knowing the spiel ever so well, would routinely mouth the first sentence with a slight alteration, *"In the event of an attack during tonight's movie… run like hell!"*

On one occasion, a howitzer at the nearby Army base was providing the nightly H&I fire when a "short round" exploded soon after it was fired creating a sound similar to an in-coming mortar. There was an immediate response at the theater as hundreds of GIs scampered to the ground leaving a cloud of dust in the air. Maybe that's how the theater got its name.

---

[1] The canopy was installed to provide moviegoers a dry environment during the rainy monsoon season. Until then, the open-air arena was called the *Starlite Theater.*

The theater was also used for touring USO[1] shows by placing a flatbed trailer in front of the screen for use as a stage. The shows that featured female singers and dancers were especially well attended – more so if the girls were "round-eyed," a term many GIs used to describe females who were not of Asian ancestry. USO performers looked forward to Nha Trang visits because between shows they could enjoy our famous beach. When the shapely females sunbathed in their skimpy bikinis, it usually caused a frenzy at the beach.

★★★★★

Among the many health risks in Vietnam (other than being a war zone) was Malaria, an infectious disease transmitted by mosquitoes. The symptoms of Malaria include fever, sweats, chills, headache, body aches, and malaise. Under certain circumstances, the disease could be fatal. I was told if I should ever come down with Malaria, death would be a blessing.

An anti-Malaria pill, dispensed in the chow hall every Monday morning, was our prime defense to thwart off this hideous disease. Taking the pill was on the honor system – no one would individually monitor this weekly ritual. Some GIs foolishly opted not to indulge in this prescription and take their chances with the disease.

It wasn't the taste of the pill that everyone despised... it was the side effect – *diarrhea!* Not a subtle, gentle nature call... but a sudden onslaught that provoked a foot race to the nearest latrine.

---

[1] The United Service Organizations (USO) is a private, nonprofit organization whose mission is to support the Armed Forces by providing morale, welfare and recreation-type services.

More times than not, the pill would win as evidenced by the victim's sudden slower pace to the can.

I discovered breaking the pill into halves and taking a half-pill at two consecutive meals could lessen the side effects. Anyone returning from Vietnam could not donate blood for two years due to the malaria risk.

*****

I had put off the inevitable for as long as I could – Sgt. Johns told me I was past due for a haircut. I was paranoid about a haircut because all barbers on base were Vietnamese and, at that time, I was cynical about any Asian… especially one standing behind me with a straight razor. I had to succumb to my fear and get it over with.

I entered the barbershop on base to discover the barbers were all females which eased my paranoia a bit. The shop had three barber chairs with a long mirror on the wall facing the chairs. The place reeked with a sweet aroma like a combination of perfume and hair tonic. The first two chairs were occupied so I went to the last one. The woman never spoke a word and immediately tied a cape around my neck and began the cut with scissors and a comb. I kept a watchful eye in the mirror the whole time and was prepared to make a run for it if needed.

Surprisingly, the experience went rather well. The young woman appeared to know what she was doing and never looked threatening – my most intense moment was when she shaved the back of my neck with a razor.

When I thought the haircut was finished, I started to get out of the chair and she pulled me back. I was totally unprepared for what happened next and it created a brief moment of fear – she took hold of my chin with one hand and my head with the other and *"SNAP!"* – she popped my neck much like a chiropractor would do. She then popped the other side in the same manner.

After my "adjustment," she leaned me forward in the chair and began thumping my upper back and shoulders with her cupped hands making a slapping sound. She completed the haircut by splashing my neck with the sweet tonic that lingered for hours. The haircut and unexpected massage[1] were very invigorating. Even better, the treatments were extremely affordable – the whole tab was a whopping forty cents.

★★★★★

When a FAC reported a stronghold of Viet Cong located on the mountain range southwest of the airfield, my suspicions about that area being a prime location to lob mortars onto the airbase was confirmed. The base upgraded to Yellow Alert, which meant an attack was imminent. All movies were cancelled and the Chapel services were postponed. None of the Vietnamese workers, not even the mamasans, showed up for work the next day – a sure bet something was about to happen.

The Viet Cong usually took advantage of the nighttime hours to stage their attacks on the airbase. When under attack, all lights on the airbase were extinguished to deny the VC any visual reference points. We were told to be attentive and to be ready for anything. It was that last part that bothered me the most.

I placed my flak vest and helmet at the foot of my bunk and was still concerned about being in the top berth. My sleep was

---

[1] These amenities were customary and performed without charge or consent.

sporadic and shallow due to the anxiety of the situation. I kept a keen ear to any unusual sounds but remembered something an old-timer once said, *"It's the one you don't hear that'll getcha!"*

I was amazed that a person with such little time in-country like myself could identify so readily the sound of a detonating mortar. On that particular night, I was in my bunk reading by the light of a small lamp at the head of my bed. The resonance of the blast was different from anything else I'd ever heard. That night there was no mistaking what I heard or that we were under attack.

When the first round hit, I instinctively lunged off the top bunk hitting the hard concrete floor. I stood up just long enough to retrieve my vest and helmet. I grabbed my sleeping roommate by his shirt and literally dragged him off the bunk onto the floor next to me. He woke up cursing until he realized what was happening.

We heard the barracks chief yell, *"Turn off that damn light…NOW!"* I then realized my reading light was still on so I jerked the lamp's electrical cord pulling the whole lamp off the shelf onto the floor. My light was out – permanently.

The second and third mortar detonated and the sound was getting closer! The sergeant at the equipment counter was right – I wanted to crawl under my steel helmet for protection. We hunkered facedown on the floor as more mortars fell from the sky. I hoped their targets were aircraft on the flightline and not servicemen in the barracks – the anxiety was unbearable.

After more than a dozen hits, everything got quiet. The roar of Spooky's[1] miniguns seeking revenge soon broke the silence. Remembering the statement from the in-briefing that a lull in the assault doesn't mean it's over, I didn't dare get up. After about ninety minutes, a security policeman in  a jeep drove down the roadway announcing the all-clear signal using a powered megaphone. I wondered how he knew that. The barracks slowly came back to life as the lights came back on and GIs started moving about. To our relief, there were no causalities... except for my reading lamp.

At daybreak, the full battle damage was assessed. As suspected,

 the VC had dropped mortars on the flightline hoping to inflict damage to the aircrafts, but only one aircraft took a direct hit. A maintenance vehicle was hit along with a nearby storage building. Most aircraft were well protected by the revetments that surrounded three sides of each airplane.

Later that day, 105mm Howitzers[2] began shelling the hillside relentlessly, but the FACs continued to report enemy activity in the area. The shelling went on for several days until an air strike was declared. A Bird Dog spotted the suspected target with his "Willie

---

[1]   *"Spooky"* was the radio call sign for an AC-47 gunship used for close air support.
[2]   A 105mm Howitzer is a light field-artillery weapon with an effective range of seven miles.

Pete[1]" rockets while three A1-E *Skyraiders*[2], laden with several five-hundred pound bombs, circled overhead. Systematically, each *Skyraider* would peel away from the formation and dive bomb the target resulting in a violent explosion that created a visual shock wave and rattled the hillside. A few times the pilots did a victory roll during the climb-out following a bomb run. Everyone on base had a ringside seat for this air attack which could easily be seen, felt, and heard.

The reality of this bombing was an eye-opener to me. What I was seeing wasn't a Hollywood movie, newsreel or videotape. That

Smoke cloud from bombs

was *real* and I was witnessing it firsthand. I had to remind myself that each time a bomb exploded, most likely human lives were being lost. I felt that I had aged a few years in one afternoon.

✱✱✱✱✱

Each month there was a mandatory group-gathering of all squadron personnel called a "Commander's Call." Lt. Col. Feuerriegel, our Squadron Commander, frequently held his Commander's Calls at the beach. The event took on a festive atmosphere by including a huge charcoal grill full of steaks and an

---

[1]   "*Willie Pete*" is the nickname for a white phosphorous smoke rocket.
[2]   A *Skyraider* was a WWII vintage propeller-driven aircraft that could carry up to 8,000 lb of ordnance on 15 external hard-points including bombs, mine dispensers, rockets, or gun pods.

abundant amount of beer and sodas iced down in a utility trailer. The uniform-of-the-day was officially announced as *"swim suits"* and Lt. Col. Feuerriegel had his silver oak leaf rank pinned to his.

There was a semi-formal agenda where the Colonel made announcements, told a few jokes, and recognized people for their accomplishments. It was a time for good eats and some silly fun. The First Sergeant[1] routinely got doused in the ocean regardless of what uniform he was wearing. The Commander's call lasted most all afternoon and was a great morale booster that took our minds far away from the war.

★★★★★

The Fourth of July came and went with little fanfare – it was a routine day with no celebration whatsoever. I supposed the war couldn't pause just to recognize a stateside holiday. I couldn't help but think about all the barbecues, watermelons, fireworks, and family gatherings that were occurring back home and hoped everyone was grateful for that opportunity. I also hoped they realized we were in Vietnam and defending their freedom to celebrate.

I reached another milestone of sorts eight days later on July 12 when I legally became an adult. It was my twenty-first birthday, something I had been anticipating for years. I never dreamed I'd celebrate that long-awaited day in Vietnam. Now that it had arrived, it really wasn't a big deal. I didn't feel any different from the day before and I surely didn't look any different. Except for

---

[1] The title "First Sergeant" is not a rank, but a special duty held by a senior enlisted member of a military unit who reports directly to the unit commander.

receiving a few birthday cards from the family and scrumptious homemade brownies from Barbara, it was just another day.

A Vietnamese custom that I admired was that human life begins at conception, so a newborn child was considered nine months old at birth – the time in the womb was accountable. So in one sense, I had actually turned twenty-one nine months ago.

The only privilege I gained by being a legal adult was the entitlement to purchase alcoholic beverages… but I seldom did. I've always found it strange and somewhat of a paradox that a serviceman less than twenty-one years of age can be drafted into the Armed Forces and fight (and possibly die) for his country…but that same person couldn't buy himself a beer.

★★★★★

In early August, I finally received my long-awaited promotion orders. The effective date on the orders was the first day of June. *I had been an Airman First Class for more than a month and didn't know it!* Upon receiving that news, I immediately changed into a set of my new jungle fatigues which already had two stripes sewn on each sleeve. It felt so good… my paranoia about being a "mosquito wing" was finally over!

I was also anticipating a pay raise but I realized that my salary for the last two paydays already included my pay increase. In addition, I was benefiting from being in Vietnam in terms of monetary compensation – tax-free pay, combat pay, hazardous duty pay, overseas pay, and family separation pay. Those perks along with my regular wages brought my salary up to $268 per month. I sent Barbara a $200 money order each month and held back the balance for myself. Except for incidentals and toiletries, I had no mandatory purchases so I saved the bulk of my portion[1].

The first of each month was payday and each GI was paid directly with MPC. There was also an MPC-to-Piaster exchange but once you made the transaction, there was no reverse exchange

available. The official exchange rate was between 80 to 90 Piaster per dollar. However, the US Government, in an effort to bolster the local economy, gave GIs one 118 Piaster to one dollar. I typically exchanged about $9.00 to Piaster for Bá Klaum's mamasan fee.

*****

An additional duty for the late shift crew was to load launchers and rockets on a certain O-2A aircraft. Every evening before dark we had to hang a LAU-59 rocket launcher under each wing of Col. Feuerriegel's O-2A *Skymaster*. Occasionally he instructed us to load

the launchers with con-
ventional rockets instead
of the usual smoke
rockets. Each launcher
could hold up to seven
rockets that could be fired
individually or be rippled
off in a single salvo.

---

[1] With my accumulated savings, I later purchased a component stereo system and a 35mm camera.

The *Skymaster* would remain on alert throughout the night. The radio call sign was *"Cagey"* which was reserved for the current TASS Commander. The following morning, if the aircraft didn't fly, the rockets would be downloaded and the launchers removed.

Most nights the aircraft never left the revetment. But on one particular night during a Yellow Alert, Col. Feuerriegel and another officer scrambled the *Skymaster,* loaded with conventional rockets, to provide air support. They returned in less than an hour with two empty launchers and seemed very jovial over their outcome. They didn't discuss any details of their mission but their smiles told everyone it was more than successful. I overheard the Commander say to his flight companion, *"I'll buy the next round of drinks at the Club!"*

✶✶✶✶✶

My first trip to downtown Nha Trang was momentous. When security conditions allowed it, the Air Force provided scheduled bus service to the downtown area. Each bus had chicken wire over the windows just like the buses at Cam Ranh – and for the same reason. Many senior NCOs lodged in secured villas in town because of insufficient on-base facilities and they relied on the bus service regularly.

Carl Frost, a friend from the electric shop, and I decided to make our first venture to town. We boarded the bus next to the Dustbowl Theater and soon we were underway. The bus exited the airbase at the main gate and drove north on Beach Road. The roadway was packed mostly with two-wheeled scooters and bicycles – all of which had several riders in addition to their over-sized cargo. A few privately owned cars were seen, but the larger vehicles were mostly military jeeps and trucks.

It was a pleasant drive along the palm-lined shoreline – the ocean was calm and clear. The view changed dramatically when we turned away from the beach and took a road toward town.

Downtown Nha Trang was a bustling community that had an interesting diversity of people, churches, schools, and merchants. The townspeople were a fascinating blend of several harmonious cultures and religions as evidenced by the varied churches and shrines.

People were everywhere[1] and most of them were on the move

using all kinds of vehicles. A popular vehicle was a cyclo – a covered carriage propelled by pedal-power from a single driver at the rear of the vehicle. U. S. servicemen were forbidden to ride in cyclos because the operator was behind the carriage and out of sight from his clients. Intersections were without traffic signals so each had to be negotiated with caution.

Commerce was plentiful, especially in the heart of the city with its stores, shops, and markets. The Nha Trang Hotel offered lodging with its three-storied building and amenities that included a rooftop

---

[1] In 1968, Nha Trang's population was about 65,000.

swimming pool[1]. The hotel had seen better years and was a remnant of its once elegant self.

There was hardly any loitering observed except for children on the street and a few prostitutes. Vietnamese kids were known to swarm servicemen and, in the mayhem, slit the hip pocket of the unsuspecting GI and make off with his wallet. For that reason, Carl and I carried our wallets in our shirt pocket.

Sadly, many Vietnamese children were fathered by U.S. soldiers and were known unaffectionately as *Amerasians*. Their genetics produced noticeably different appearances that led them to become social outcasts early in their lives. The merciless taunting by other children contributed to many Amerasians dropping out of school after only a few years.

Carl and I exited the bus on Doc Lop Street and went into the downtown USO club. Admittedly, I had high anxiety about being in town. The club felt like a sanctuary because it isolated me from the realism of the world just beyond the doors. We both bought a tepid Coke and struck up a conversation with another serviceman there. He offered us some advice about interacting with the local Vietnamese: keep a low profile, don't be boisterous, don't flash around a lot of money, and finally, don't patronize the "boom-boom" girls if you want to remain healthy.

Primed with that information, Carl and I ventured outside once again. We casually walked down the street and tried to be inconspicuous, but we were like magnets to merchants, kids, and hookers. Young boys no older than six years old were selling marijuana joints while others were soliciting clients for their "virgin

---

[1] The pool was void of water throughout my tour.

sister." We shunned them off, noticing a young woman standing in the entrance to a bar trying to entice us to buy her some "Saigon Tea[1]." When we walked past her, she became arrogant and cursed us in perfect English.

We eventually adapted to the surroundings and felt a little better about being there. We walked past an outdoor food market that produced a plethora of smells – a few being rancid. We saw a bustling train station[2] with people everywhere and the adjacent street congested with cyclos, taxies, and motor scooters.

Following our walking tour of the downtown area, Carl noticed a white statue of Buddha on a distant hilltop that overlooked the city. We thought it might be something to visit so we took a taxi to the statue. The driver identified our destination as Long Song Pagoda and freely took MPC for the fare. Local merchants were not suppose to accept MPC as currency – but most did anyway.

The statue was huge – the largest in Vietnam – and it dominated the local landscape. To the right of the statue and down the hillside was a Buddhist temple, and on a pole above the temple was a swastika – which created some concern because of its

---

[1] Saigon Tea referred to what the bar girls drank when they encouraged a lonely soldier to buy them a drink. She would remain cozy with the GI until he stopped buying the expensive non-alcoholic "tea."

[2] The French originally built a 1,074-mile railway system that ran from Haiphong down the full length of the country through Nha Trang and ending in Saigon.

association with Nazi Germany[1]. Carl and I walked up the steps to the shrine and found many lit candles and the sweet aroma of incense. The floor was spotless and highly polished, and there was a massive metal gong suspended from the ceiling with a horizontal swinging timber to sound it.

No sooner than we had arrived, a Buddhist monk came out of nowhere and began angrily addressing us in words we didn't understand – maybe we weren't suppose to be there. After a while, we realized he was upset over our boots – it was customary to remove footwear when in the temple. We took off our boots and the monk instantly became the perfect host, eager to show us the shrine – a lot of smiling, bowing, and head nodding took place.

Afterwards, we put on our boots and climbed more steps to the statue. The snow-white icon dwarfed anyone standing beside it, and the concrete edifice was riddled with dimples – most likely created by gunshot. The area was immaculately clean with red Cannas lilies blooming around the perimeter. Directly in front of the Buddha was a wide set of stairs that flared out away from the statue. On each side of the steps were intricate

sculptures of dragons symbolically offering protection to the Buddha. The view toward downtown and our airbase was spectacular.

---

[1] Although the Swastika is often synonymous with the Nazi movement of the 20th century, it was widely used in ancient times as a symbol of prosperity and good fortune.

Carl and I lounged in the statue's broad shadow while enjoying the breeze from the nearby ocean. The break gave me a moment to digest all that I had encountered in the past two hours. That was my first experience in a dissimilar culture – the inhabitants looked different, spoke a different language, and most believed in a different deity. I most certainly was in the minority and it felt strange and a bit unnerving.

U. S. Servicemen were encouraged to embrace the Vietnamese culture by mingling with the people and honoring their customs and beliefs. For the most part, I found the people in Nha Trang to be warm, friendly, and very family oriented.

During those pensive moments, I came to realize a most profound aspect of my situation – I was a temporary guest in their country, and I would eventually be returning to my own culture to actively pursue the "American Dream." That war-torn country was their homeland and most Vietnamese would most likely never leave it.  For the first time I began to feel remorse over the fact the Vietnamese were entailed in a war that threatened their freedom and their way of life. I began to realize a new perspective and, in doing so, gained an unexpected appreciation for their courageous plight.

After about an hour, Carl and I again took a taxi back to downtown. We went into a camera shop and Carl looked for a particular camera adapter, which they didn't have. Then we entered an apparel store and the Vietnamese proprietor greeted us at the entrance with an enormous smile. I purchased a blue satin oriental kimono as a gift for Barbara hoping I had guessed the right size.

After a full day of seeing the sights, I became more at ease in my unfamiliar surroundings – I never felt threatened or endangered in any way. Reluctantly, Carl and I boarded the military bus to take us back to the airbase. It had been an incredible experience – one that would linger for decades.

★★★★★

One of our O-1E Bird Dogs had to make a crash landing in a rice field after small-arms fire riddled the wing's fuel tank. After a "*Mayday*[1]" call on the radio, the two crewmembers were promptly rescued by a helicopter and the ruins of the aircraft were airlifted back to the squadron. The wings were destroyed in the crash and all that remained was the fuselage, rudder, and elevator.

I was surprised to learn that our squadron rebuilt crashed aircraft using a supply of aircraft parts that included wings, engines,

rudders, and landing gears. When an aircraft was restored, it was given the identical tail number of the original one. This strategy kept the squadron's aircraft inventory mostly intact – due to this rebuilding effort, we seldom lost an aircraft.

---

[1] "*Mayday*" is a universal distress call.

When it came time to repair the armament circuitry of the recently crashed aircraft, Sgt. Johns approached me about performing this task. Without hesitation, I eagerly volunteered. I was pleased for two reasons – first, rewiring the Bird Dog would be challenging and would provide an opportunity for me to use some of my dormant electrical skills. It would also be a welcomed departure from the mundane tasks of performing preventative maintenance. Secondly, the assignment of this special job led me to believe Sgt. Johns had confidence in my ability.

I worked strenuously for two days in the hot sun routing wires throughout the aircraft and making connections to the armament panel – all the while hoping I hadn't accepted an assignment that was beyond my capability. It was late on the second night that I completed the wiring and was ready to check out the system. Much to my disappointment, the system didn't work – the firing voltage never appeared at the launchers when the trigger was pulled in the cockpit. In desperation I rechecked all the wiring against the schematics in the Tech Order[1] and everything seemed to be connected properly... but it just didn't work.

The next morning, I dejectedly reported back to the work center. When Sgt. Johns saw me he asked, *"You're back...you got everything working?"* I replied, *"No sir, I hit a snag. I'll need to spend some more time with that armament circuit."* I suppose Sgt. Johns noticed my frustration and said, *"Take a break from the job... you've been going at it pretty steadily for a couple of days and sometimes it's helpful not to think about it for a while."* That's precisely what made Sgt. Johns such a good

---

[1]   A *Technical Order* (TO) is a manual that provides clear and concise instructions for effective operation and maintenance of an aircraft or other systems within the Air Force.

boss – he never mentioned my failure to get the job done, but instead offered me support that I could do it with enough time.

I took Sgt. Johns' advice and didn't go near the Bird Dog or give the problem any thought for a full day. With renewed vigor, I returned to the aircraft the following day and discovered to my absolute astonishment the armament system worked perfectly! I thought surely that Sgt. Johns must have found and fixed the problem the day before and didn't say anything about it.

When I asked Sgt. Johns, he emphatically denied making any repairs to the aircraft. We returned to the aircraft and performed a thorough check of the armament system. Again, everything performed perfectly. In exasperation, I exclaimed, *"Things don't just fix themselves! I'm telling you this system was dead in the water just two days ago... but today it's fine."* Sgt. Johns then helped me analyze the dilemma by asking, *"What's different about today? What are you doing now that you didn't do two days ago? Is there a common denominator somewhere? What about the voltmeter... are you using the same one?"*

It was like a revelation – the voltmeter! A defective voltmeter would give a bogus indication that a problem exists in the aircraft. Why didn't I think of that? I replied to Sgt. Johns, *"I'll bet you're right. I'd say there's a good chance that one of the three voltmeters we have in the shop is kaput."*

We returned to the shop to find my prediction was right – a blown fuse in one of the voltmeters prevented the device from working properly. It was that inoperative meter I used during my first attempt to check out the system. I had wired the Bird Dog correctly but didn't know it because of a stupid voltmeter. Nevertheless, Sgt. Johns did praise me for the task and never mentioned my shortsightedness – again, the qualities of a good boss.

This episode taught me a lesson: When attempting to find a solution to any problem, I should avoid tunnel vision and expand my realm of thought beyond that of the immediate situation. By thinking "outside the box," more factors become obvious and lend themselves to the solution. In the meantime, I made a point to first check out the voltmeter anytime an electrical problem arose.

✶✶✶✶✶

In late August, the airbase was notified of a possible typhoon (the Pacific's equal to a hurricane) that had been brewing as a tropical depression near Manila and was now headed toward Southeast Asia. Nha Trang Airbase was a mere sixteen feet above sea level and a major typhoon, with its accompanying storm surge, could be cataclysmic and inflict more damage than any enemy action.

Contingency measures were initiated which called for the securing of any and all loose items that could be lethal if propelled by high winds. Shutters on barracks' windows were closed and tied down. Sandbags were filled and placed on everything, including the wings of all our aircraft. An evacuation plan for both personnel and aircraft was prepared and became ready to execute, based on the exact location of the storm's landfall. Speculations on the typhoon's projected path abounded, and wagers were made by many GIs as to the whereabouts of its landfall.

All coastal U.S. military installations in Vietnam sighed in relief when the full-fledged typhoon made an unexpected northwesterly turn and tracked directly toward Hong Kong where it made a devastating landfall two days later.

★★★★★

It was so reassuring to receive letters from home... to have that link to a loved one was so very special. For a brief period of time, reading my letters would remove me from my current surroundings and sweep me to a much happier place and time. My entire extended family – aunts, uncles, and cousins – were great about sending me cards and letters that offered encouragement and telling me I was in their thoughts and prayers.

I came to realize a most significant aspect about my letters home – when Barbara, my parents, or other family members received a letter from me, they were assured of my welfare only at the time of my letter – five days *previously*. Anything could have happened to me between the time I wrote the letter and the time they received the letter. When the homebound mail was delayed, it caused anxiety back home. In one way, I had the advantage because at any time I knew I was all right – they didn't.

Barbara wrote me every day, and I cherished her letters[1]. Within the squadron, I quickly became a yardstick in terms of the mail. If someone didn't get an expected letter, they'd check with me to see if the mail had been delayed. They often said, *"If Moss doesn't get mail... nobody gets mail!"* I didn't mind those comments one bit!

---

[1]   Barbara and I have re-read our daily letters to each other on the 40th anniversary of the original date of each letter.

✶✶✶✶✶

As I became adapted to my new environment and lifestyle, there was a noticeable drop in my anxiety level. I began to understand what Franklin Roosevelt once said about fear – I had been fearful over being afraid. The unknown element, which had contributed a great deal to my uneasiness, had been somewhat eliminated. My early concern about *"Would I be able to take it?"* was unfounded.

Chapter 9

Rain, Rain…Go Away!

September – November 1968

"Anything I've ever done that ultimately was
worthwhile initially scared me to death."
Betty Bender

In the News…

* *The Detroit Tigers came from behind to win the World Series over the St. Louis Cardinals. The Tigers overcame a historic three games to one deficit – only three other teams since 1900 had beaten such odds.*

* *The XIX Summer Olympiad concluded in Mexico City with the United States barely surpassing the Soviet Union in total medals won. The event was marred when two U.S. athletes, who after taking the gold and silver in the 200 meter sprint, raised a clinched fist symbolizing the Black Panther salute during the playing of the Star Spangled Banner at the award ceremony. The U.S. Olympic Committee later suspended the two athletes.*

* *In an attempt to break the stalemated Paris peace talks, President Johnson announced that all naval, air, and artillery bombardment of North Vietnam would cease on November 1. Critics proclaimed the action was to bolster Hubert Humphrey's bid for the presidency because the election was just four days away.*

* *Republican Richard Nixon defeated Hubert Humphrey in one of the closest general elections in history by just 0.7 percent of the popular vote. However, the Democrats would retain the control of Congress. Nixon's running mate for vice president was Maryland's Governor Spiro T. Agnew.*

* *The Ohio State Buckeyes finished a perfect season (10-0-0) and were the consensus national NCAA football champions for 1968. Meanwhile the*

coveted Heisman Trophy went to USC running back O.J. Simpson after gaining 3,187 yards and scoring 21 touchdowns.

* The CBS news magazine "60 Minutes" premiered on CBS-TV on a Tuesday night.

* Former first lady Jacqueline Kennedy married Greek shipping magnate Aristotle Onassis.

* The Motion Picture Association of America adopted its film-rating system (G,M,R,X), ranging from "G" for "general" audiences to "X" for adult patrons only.

* On November 9, a 5.4 magnitude earthquake shook a 580,000 square-mile area of the central United States, including all or portions of 23 states. The epicenter was in south-central Illinois near the New Madrid Fault but caused only minor damage.

* After a 25-day holdout, South Vietnam agreed to participate in the Peace talks. Meanwhile, Communist troops fired upon U.S. positions from within the DMZ[1], 10 days after the November 1 announcement.

* The total number of aircraft lost over Vietnam by the U.S. now exceeded 900.

Unbelievably, the air attack on the hillside didn't eradicate the VC as more activity was once again reported. My hunch was that more insurgents arrived on the hillside after the bombardment. The next morning, the din of several propeller-driven aircraft approached the area from the northwest over the estuary of the river. Four C-130

---

[1] The Demilitarized Zone (DMZ) was a neutral area 5km on each side of the Ben Hai River near the 17th paraell. This demarcation line, estblished by the Geneva Accords on July 21, 1954, geographically divided the country into North and South Vietnam.

Hercules cargo aircraft flew in a staggered formation from our right to left toward the hillside – all with their rear cargo doors wide open. As the first aircraft approached the suspected area, several silver canisters rolled out of the rear door and each plummeted end-over-end to the ground. Upon impact, each canister exploded in an enormous fireball eruption accompanied by a cloud of smoke. Each C-130 delivered the same token of hell and in less than  two minutes, the entire hillside was a blazing inferno with tons of smoke. The firestorm continued well into the late afternoon and by nightfall, spotty fires could still be seen.

I immediately recognized the ordinance as napalm[1] – a subject matter taught in Tech School. A single firebomb consisted of 100 gallons of JP-4 jet fuel mixed with a thickener to create a sticky, incendiary gel. It was used extensively to eradicate enemy stronghold positions, especially ones that were dug into the landscape. Oddly, the fireball wasn't the only menace – suffocation was also a threat. When a firebomb detonated near a cave or tunnel, the enormous gulp of combustion would pull the oxygen out of the area and suffocate anyone inside. To its critics, napalm represented the fiery essence of all that was horrible about the war in Vietnam.

---

[1] First developed at Harvard University in the early 1940's, napalm was formulated by mixing a powdered aluminum soap of naphthalene with palmitate – hence napalm.

Indeed, napalm was a horrendous weapon that caused a great deal of hurt – all too often to innocent civilians. But as I watched that incredible occurrence, I felt myself becoming calloused toward the fact that people were suffering by that hideous act of war. I had slowly acquired a *"Better them than me"* attitude that began to haunt me. Was I being victimized so soon by the war? I pondered the matter for some time and concluded I must make a conscientious effort to combat that attitude. My core values had to be stronger. I prayed for strength to resist that belligerent mentality that so many servicemen had unintentionally acquired.

The next day, the Yellow Alert was cancelled and things slowly returned to normal. But not for long – despite all the bombardment, new activity was again spotted on the hillside. Engaging the enemy with ground troops was deemed necessary, and a company of Korean soldiers was dispatched to the hillside. ROK[1] soldiers were tough as nails and utterly ruthless – they *never* took prisoners. The battle was over in no time with a body count of 267 Viet Cong insurgents dead with not a single ROK casualty. They found the hillside honeycombed with a network of underground tunnels that afforded a means of retreat when the bombing occurred. Afterwards, everything on the airbase returned to normal alert status – the current battle was over... for now.

Shortly after midnight two days later, the base sirens began heralding as enemy mortars began to besiege the area. Unlike the previous covert "hit and run" attacks, that one was different. It was a concerted offensive by many Viet Cong and lasted well into the daylight hours. Perhaps that was a retaliatory grudge by the VC for our recent napalm attack.

---

[1] Republic of Korea

The first barrage of about thirty rounds of 82mm mortars were aimed at our airbase but many overshot their target and detonated in a Vietnamese community northwest of the airfield. *The Pacific Stars and Stripes* reported the attack inflicted twenty-one civilian casualties and enemy gunners also shelled downtown Nha Trang with several rounds of recoilless rifle cannons. The assault caused considerable damage and wounded seventeen Allied soldiers along with a Vietnamese policeman. For me, that was the most intense attack I had experienced since being in Vietnam.

★★★★★

My job in the armament work center quickly became routine and didn't offer much of a challenge, neither mentally nor physically. To overcome this drudgery, I took extra effort to thoroughly learn the electrical circuitry of the aircrafts and became somewhat of an authority when troubleshooting any electrical issues. I enjoyed this advantage and it earned me a degree of respect from even the "old timers" in the squadron. On a few occasions my skills provided me with immunity from the dreaded base beautification[1] detail.

I felt myself becoming stagnant in my chosen field of electronics – the career that I planned to pursue following my Air Force duty. I enrolled in a correspondence course in electronics and studied the curriculum diligently. The disadvantage with any correspondence study was the pure theory aspect with no "hands-on" opportunities whatsoever.

---

[1] Base beautification was a detail that required junior enlisted GIs to perform menial tasks such as painting, trash removal, and cleaning.

I continued to envy my roommate's assignment in the airborne communication work center – a job that he deplored. He would often request my help when troubleshooting an ailing radio. I jumped at those opportunities and occasionally spent too many hours away from my assigned work – to the extent that Sgt. Johns once had to tactfully remind me that I worked for him in the armament work center.

★★★★★

The monsoon season began in mid-September and it proved to be very disheartening. Low-hanging gray clouds that lingered for three months brought incessant rainfall ranging from a light mist to heavy downpours, but never completely dry conditions. Monsoon rains also caused the flooding of lowlands near the river delta.

The humidity hovered near one hundred percent and the thick clammy air dampened everything. The condition was much like a sauna – extremely hot and humid. Everyone was constantly damp from either the rain or perspiration. To prevent metal wristwatches from reacting with body sweat and skin oil, special watch pads designed to cover the back of a wristwatch were used – otherwise the watch would make a telltale green splotch on the wearer's skin.

I thought the rain would cool things down but I was wrong – the clouds prevented any radiant cooling and acted like a thermal blanket. That type of weather was very conducive for the growth of fungi – in the form of mildew on objects or on the body as athletes' foot and jock itch. I managed to avoid the latter by using absorbent powder and drying off as much as possible after bathing.

The mamasans despised the monsoon season because the clothes they washed wouldn't completely dry. There's something inherently wrong with using a clean towel that's already damp before it's used. Temporary clotheslines were strung inside the barracks but didn't help much. Ironing dried the clothes somewhat but nobody expected Bá Klaum to iron every article of clothing. I really detested damp underwear (many GIs wore none for that reason) so I placed a continuously burning light bulb in my metal locker to help dry my clothes. It worked to a degree but it was a trade off – my locker became a mini oven and contributed to the already high temperature.

The monsoon[1] was created by the seasonal change of wind direction caused by moisture-laden air over the oceans being drawn toward land. The air cools as it ascends the slopes of the mountain which makes the atmosphere incapable of retaining moisture, resulting in heavy rainfall.

The relentless rain caused serious flooding that curtailed many activities on base. Church was cancelled several times because of standing water in the sanctuary (the organ survived the deluge). Our area in the armament shop flooded but work continued as usual. Everyone tromped around with wet feet because our jungle boots were not waterproof.

The monsoon also had an impact on the war by frequently grounding our aircraft due to the low visibility. During marginally overcast days, some bolder FACs ventured out looking for "glory holes" – breaks in the overcast that would permit fighter jets to penetrate the cloud cover for an air strike. FACs maneuvering in low visibility weather did so at the risk of striking obscured hillsides – an unyielding opponent known as a "rock filled cloud."

---

[1]   *"Monsoon"* is derived from the Arabic word meaning *"Season."*

The Viet Cong used the monsoon season as an opportunity to move about virtually undetected and, when the clouds finally lifted, we had to deal with new enemy strongholds and increased troop strength.

The only advantage I found about the monsoon season was the brilliant rainbows it occasionally created – a magnificent display of vivid colors that sometimes made a complete arch in the sky. For me, this spectacle had a deep religious connotation that provided hope and a promise for a better tomorrow.

✶✶✶✶✶

Whenever I worked the late shift, a flashlight was normally required to complete many tasks and that quickly became a frustrating annoyance to me. During one particular procedure, the firing voltage of each rocket launcher had to be verified using a voltmeter. It was awkward holding a voltmeter and a flashlight while probing the launcher's firing contactor, and many times I held the flashlight in my teeth.

That dilemma prompted me to fabricate a device that used a small lamp similar to the ones used on an aircraft's instrument panel. The gadget was like a fat pencil with a pointed probe at one end and the lamp at the other. A coiled wire grounded the probe to the aircraft using an alligator clip. The operation was really simple – when voltage was present, the lamp illuminated. By using my "Rocket Fire Test Probe," the need of a flashlight and voltmeter was eliminated and the probe even worked better at night. Sgt. Johns encouraged me to submit my device to the Air Force Suggestion Program, which I did – and then I promptly put it out of my mind.

✴✴✴✴✴

A base-wide project to replace all the rusty window screens on the barracks got underway in September. The task was being performed by a crew of Vietnamese men who must have been paid by the hour rather than by the job because they worked at an unhurried and leisurely pace.

After my barracks was rescreened, I discovered my new wind-up alarm clock was missing – it had been on a small shelf at the head of my bunk. I suppose it had been too tempting for a worker not to slip it into his pocket unnoticed. I reported the theft to the Security Police and told them that my name and service number were scratched on the back of the clock. They didn't offer any encouragement of ever recovering the stolen item, but they did complete an incident report. The next day I purchased a replacement clock at the exchange – a wind-up clock was more dependable than an electric one because the electrical power was often sporadic and unreliable.

✴✴✴✴✴

An unannounced MPC exchange was carried out in September. The whole airbase was put on a lockdown and on-base merchants were not allowed to open for business until the new MPC was issued. That was an annoyance that everyone had to endure.

An exchange station was set up in the front area of our squadron and everyone surrendered their old MPC for a like amount of new MPC. Each denomination's color, layout, and portrait changed, so the new MPC was noticeably different except for the physical size.

I began to understand the necessity for MPC – the U.S. dollar was a premium commodity in the local Vietnamese financial market and contributed greatly to the inflation of the economy. The use of MPC, instead of actual greenback dollars, provided a means to keep U.S. currency from infiltrating the local economy. The periodic exchange of MPC would render the old MPC absolutely worthless and merchants who accepted MPC would be holding valueless money. That was an incentive for merchants not to accept MPC as legal tender – despite that risk, most shop owners freely took MPC as payment.

✱✱✱✱✱

As I was returning to the barracks one afternoon, Bá Klaum met me in the doorway and she looked distressed. She said in a whimper, *"Mamasan numba ten[1]."* My first thought was that she was sick until she showed me a nasty burn on the outside of her right arm above her wrist. The outline of the reddened area was in the shape of her electric  iron. When I saw her injury I remarked, *"Ow, that's gotta hurt!"*

I sat her down on my bunk and began to rummage through my first aid kit for any burn ointment. I extended her arm and gently pushed back the sleeve of her blouse to fully expose the affected area. When I applied the lotion to the burn, she cringed with pain. Remembering how my Mom would make things feel better when I

---

[1] *"Number ten"* was the worst of anything while *"Number one"* was the best of anything.

skinned a knee or burned myself as a child, I instinctively pursed my lips and began to blow on her burn in the same manner. I wondered if she ever did that with her own children.

It felt odd being a caregiver to Bá Klaum – a person who labored relentlessly every day and who couldn't even speak my language. I came to realize she could hurt and feel pain just like anyone else. I wondered if her feelings could be hurt just as easily.

After a while, the ointment began to soothe her burn and the pain apparently diminished because she exclaimed, *"Bá Klaum numba one!"* I gave her the tube of ointment in case she needed to reapply some lotion later. She returned to her chores and never made mention of the mishap again. A few weeks after the incident, I noticed a distinguishable scar on her arm.

✶✶✶✶✶

I finally discovered what those yellow and black ribbon streamers on many GI's fatigues signified – those lucky dogs were going home soon! There was an unspoken hierarchy of respect among the enlisted GIs that centered around time-in-country more so than rank. The "short-timer's ribbon" told everyone that you had acquired revered status and were basically untouchable.

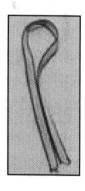

The ribbon itself was actually the yellow and black ribbon from a Seagram's VO whisky bottle and indicated the wearer had less than thirty days left in Vietnam. With less than ten days left, the wearer was entitled to tie the ribbon in a bow to indicate he had *"Single Digit Fidgets."* That tradition was, of course, not officially sanctioned by the Air Force. But because it boosted morale, the short-timers ribbon was tolerated even though it violated the official uniform regulations. A departing GI from the instrument shop gave me his ribbon and I stored it in my locker for safekeeping. I could start wearing it on April 21, 1969, which was more than eight months away!

I gained an appreciation for knowing the exact date of my departure. In previous wars and conflicts, the U.S. soldier had no idea when he'd get to go home. Typically he stayed until the war was over… or until he got injured or killed, whichever came first.

✷✷✷✷✷

In September, I received a bulging letter from my cousin Bonnie. She had enclosed a brief letter and an item that really surprised me – a Saint Christopher medal on a necklace chain. Saint Christopher is generally thought of as the patron saint of travelers. Bonnie and her whole extended family were staunch Baptists and the medal was obviously Catholic. Her letter made only a brief mention of the medal without any explanation.

Looking at the medal brought back memories of my childhood. Our neighbor next door was a Catholic family with seven children – all wore Catholic medals including one of Saint Christopher attached to their shirts with safety pins. As an only child, I spent a lot of time next door and, for a while, I too wore medals like my playmates until my Grandmother confiscated them.

Ricky, the fourth male in their family, was near my age and as youngsters, we spent countless hours playing "Army"– we had all the regalia to look like real GI Joes. Ironically, a decade later it would be the real thing[1] and a great deal different from our playful childhood pastime.

Being a lifelong Methodist, I seldom acknowledged any Catholic symbols. However, I figured wearing a Saint Christopher medal surely wouldn't hurt anything, so I placed the necklace around my neck along with my dog tags. A few days later, Bá Klaum was delighted when she noticed my medal. She showed me her Saint Christopher medal she had around her neck and said, *"Same."* I wore the medal for several weeks until the heat and high humidity discolored it and it caused a green stain to appear around my neck.

✳✳✳✳✳

After serving a minimum of six months in-country, U.S. Servicemen were entitled to a sabbatical called "Rest and Recuperation," better known as R&R. The Armed Forces would send GIs to a variety of locations free of charge for a brief six-day escape.

Some of the more popular destinations were Tokyo, Sydney, Hong Kong, Bangkok, and Honolulu. Most of the married servicemen chose Honolulu to reunite with their spouses for that brief time. Barbara and I were excited for that opportunity, and I put in my request for a Hawaiian R&R for sometime in January. Our trip was the hot topic in our daily letters and became a new milestone for both of us. The idea of being in a South Pacific

---

[1] Ricky served time in Vietnam with the 101st Airborne. He was wounded in July 1970 and spent a year recuperating at Walter Reid Hospital in Bethesda, MD. He passed away in April 2009 due to the long-term complications of his injuries.

paradise was eclipsed by the thought of being with my bride once again, even if it was for a fleeting six days.

*****

A new senior sergeant arrived at the armament work center – Tech Sgt. James Baker from Oxnard, California. He had more time-in-rank than Sgt. Johns so, by protocol, he became the new NCOIC of the work center, regardless of his lack of knowledge of our operations. Sgt. Johns was all too ready to give up the throne – he was ready to go home.

Sgt. Baker, a stout man originally from Jessup, Georgia, was humble and friendly. He was noticeably uncomfortable with his new supervisor role and relied heavily on the experienced personnel in the work center. I wasn't too keen about this change because Sgt. Johns had been a great person to work for and he treated me with respect. He had praised my work during my mid-term written Airman's Proficiency Report (APR) with a lofty rating I more than likely didn't deserve.

Eventually, Sgt. Baker and I became friends and he earned my respect as a supervisor. However, I found myself unconsciously comparing Sgt. Baker's leadership style with that of Sgt. Johns – both were effective but I still held Sgt. Johns in high regard.

*****

An O1-F Bird Dog returned from a Functional Check Flight with an armament discrepancy – the pilot reported excessive vibration from a rocket launcher on the right wing. The problem was a loose sway brace that I tightened and cleared the write-up from the aircraft's logbook.

That afternoon, the new FCF pilot asked me if the problem was fixed and I told him what I had done. He said the vibration didn't sound like anything loose and wanted me to experience it firsthand. In less than an hour we were airborne over the river just northwest of downtown Nha Trang.

I listened intently for any unusual sounds but I heard nothing out of the ordinary – the roar of the engine and wind noise from the open windows could have been muffling the vibration. I asked the pilot over the intercom if he heard anything. He said on his previous FCF, he could actually feel the launcher vibrating but now it seemed to be okay. I was pleased knowing I had made the right diagnosis.

He turned the Bird Dog around and headed back toward the airbase. We were leisurely flying low over the river when we heard a sharp popping sound over the din of the engine. The pilot exclaimed, *"Did you hear that? That's ground fire!"* He didn't wait for my reply and quickly throttled up the engine, pulling the Bird Dog into a steep turning climb. Again we heard more gunfire, and the red tracer projectile was shooting past us dead ahead!

He banked the Bird Dog sharply to the right, then abruptly to the left making the aircraft a less susceptible target. I was hanging on for dear life in the rear seat not knowing the full extent of the situation. He then put the Bird Dog into a full-powered climb reaching an altitude that was out

of the small arms range. I gained an immediate appreciation for the oversized engine on the Bird Dog – the climb didn't tax the engine whatsoever.

He leveled off and backed down the throttle – once again everything returned to normal as we flew peacefully through wisps of cumulus clouds far above the ground. He finally asked, *"Are you okay back there?"* I replied, *"Yes sir, I'm still back here… but I don't know if I'm alright…I might need to change my pants."* He chuckled and said, *"Yeah, me too!"*

★★★★★

I was totally surprised at September's Commander's Call when I was presented a cash award of $20 for my Rocket Fire Test Probe suggestion. I didn't think it had any chance of being adopted. I thanked Sgt. Johns for encouraging me to submit the suggestion, and I assembled three more test probes and gave them to the other guys in our armament shop.

Then in October, I shook the hand of Lt. Col. Feuerriegel once again when he recognized me as an Honor Graduate from Tech

School at Lowery AFB. Because of the monsoon rain, the Commander's Call was held in the covered dock area. When I went forward to accept the certificate, I realized I wasn't wearing my cap and I had on my sunglasses. The Colonel gave me a stern look which unmistakably conveyed his disapproval of my appearance. At that precise moment, a photographer captured the embarrassing moment.

By far my biggest surprise came in November when it was announced that I had been selected as the "Munitions Man of the Quarter" for all of the Pacific Air Force (PACAF). I had never heard of such an award nor did I know of my nomination.

I was astounded and felt so undeserving of such an honor. The only justification I could think of was my test probe suggestion or perhaps the competition was unbelievably mediocre. I hoped a monetary award would accompany the award but such was not the case – I was told a trophy would be presented at a later date.

I became the brunt of some light-hearted ribbing because of the award. Maintenance Control issued a work order to be performed by "The Munitions Man of the Quarter" and some GIs proclaimed that I couldn't care less about the monsoon flooding because I could now "Walk on Water!"

I really didn't mind these good-natured put downs – no malice was intended. I had to make sure to stay humble with all my colleagues and to be able to laugh at myself. The recognition did impact my daily routine – I had to hold myself to a higher standard, which proved to be challenging.

✱✱✱✱✱

In mid-October, Lt. Col. Feuerriegel rotated back to the states after a seven-month assignment as the Squadron Commander. He would be sorely missed – and not just because he had beach parties. He was a decent man who was more like a father figure than a CO. He flaunted neither his rank nor his authority and never micro-managed his subordinates – something I highly respected[1].

---

[1] Col. Feuerriegel retired from the Air Force as a full Colonel in April 1974. He passed away in Prescott, Arizona on March 4, 2008 at the age of 91.

The squadron presented Lt. Col. Feuerriegel a plaque depicting flags of both U. S. and South Vietnam, a map of South Vietnam with Nha Trang highlighted, and a whimsical commemorative inscription alluding to a few of his light-hearted legacies[1].

Our new commander was Lt. Col. Joseph M. Forster[2], whose managerial style was totally opposite from that of Col. Feuerriegel. His first Commander's Call was a formal assembly held in the base Chapel instead of a casual and festive party on the beach. As expected, that event was now looked upon as drudgery instead of a festivity – indicated by the overall drop in morale and productivity of the personnel. It wasn't long before Col. Forster returned to the ways of his predecessor and things got a lot better.

*****

Much to my delight, I discovered it was possible to call home – not over a telephone line but by radio waves. A program was established consisting of licensed amateur radio operators who were interested in military communications. The program was

---

[1] That plaque is now in my possession – the Feuerriegel family graciously gave it to me after the Colonel's passing.

[2] Lieutenant Colonel Forster retired in January 1971. His decorations include two Distinguished Flying Crosses and seven Air Medals. (He shot down 9 Japanese aircraft in the Pacific Theater during WWII.) As of this writing, he lives with his wife in Arizona.

called Military Affiliate Radio System (MARS) and there was a station not far from my barracks.

Communications were sent via radio waves[1] across the ocean to  a stateside MARS station and from there, the call was placed over normal telephone circuits to its final destination with a collect call. As a general rule, MARS calls originated exclusively from Vietnam and seldom from the states.

Many times a stateside station owned by Senator Barry Goldwater in Phoenix, Arizona, was used. Volunteers manned his MARS station[2] and the Senator would absorb the cost of all collect calls – a nice deed for the Armed Forces.

To make a call, GIs had to make a reservation in advance and arrive early at the station to wait their turn. It reminded me a lot like a doctor's waiting room with chairs around the wall and a small pass-through window where your name would be announced when the connection was established. The GI would then enter a smaller room – much like a phone booth – and speak with his stateside party in semi-privacy[3] using an ordinary telephone.

Unlike a typical phone call where both parties could speak simultaneously, a MARS call was "unidirectional," meaning only one party could speak at a time. When the speaking party was through, they had to say the word *"Over"* to alert the MARS

---

[1]   The frequency was in the 15-meter band (19 Mhz).
[2]   Sen. Goldwater's MARS station operated with the call sign of "AFA7UGA."
[3]   Actually, anyone could eavesdrop on the call with any HAM radio receiver.

operators to switch their radios to the opposite mode so the other party could speak. That proved to be a bit awkward at times and often lessened an affectionate phrase… such as *"I love you, OVER."*

The radio signal used a technical mode called "single sideband" which sometimes distorted the voice. The conversation was distinguishable, but sometimes the voice wasn't recognizable. Nevertheless, it was nice to converse instantly over the radio rather than enduring a five-day hiatus using the mail.

I made monthly MARS calls to Barbara but usually spoke with her Mom. Barbara had the uncanny timing of being somewhere other than home when I called. To remedy that situation, I began calling mid afternoon in Vietnam, so the phone in Atlanta would ring before sunrise.

Forbidden topics, including troop strength, recent attacks, deployments, or any other bits of information that might benefit an eavesdropper, were not allowed to be discussed over MARS. Every GI was entitled to one five-minute MARS call every 30 days.

★★★★★

Adjacent to Nha Trang Airbase was the Army 5th Special Forces – better known as Green Berets. These guys were the real deal and tough as steel. I was humbled to be among the real warriors of the war and it made me appreciate the style of living afforded to me by being assigned to a secure airbase.

Access between the two military installations was unrestricted and the boundary was unmistakable – the airbase had improved roads, permanent dwellings, and nice aesthetics while the Army camp had muddy roads, lots of tents, and it looked like… well, a camp.

What the camp had that the airbase didn't have was a *Playboy Club*. When I first heard about it, my mind conjured up visions of the obvious, but it wasn't anything near what one might expect from the name. It was, however, a very popular gathering spot that served great food – anything from grilled cheese sandwiches to sirloin steaks.

To purchase items at the club, "chits" were sold at the front entrance and could be redeemed inside for food and drink, which beat anything we had at the airbase. Many Air Force GIs were among its regular patrons. The Green Berets didn't  seem to mind the intermingling of our two outfits even though occasionally they'd subtly flaunt their superiority over us "fly boys."

The *Playboy Club* was officially labeled a Personnel Coming Off Duty (PCOD) lounge but it evolved into a well-liked nightspot. At times, they'd offer some decent live entertainment – musical groups featuring oriental female singers, who were often monetarily enticed by the show-goers to do a strip tease. A rocket and mortar attack destroyed the club in 1965 but it was quickly rebuilt.

✶✶✶✶✶

Occasionally I would find items under my pillow placed there by Bá Klaum – not valuables, but empty boxes or bottles of things she needed. These items included shampoo, washing powder, body lotion, and other such sundries. I'd make the purchase the next day at the Base Exchange and discreetly give her the items free of charge. I was content to provide her with these requested items and she was humble and grateful for the gifts. The only time I refused to participate was when I found a feminine hygiene product under my pillow. This exchange continued with Bá Klaum throughout my tour, and I never mentioned it to anyone.

One day I noticed Bá Klaum was sitting on the floor and pinching the bridge of her nose. I asked her what was wrong and she replied, *"Bá Klaum boo coop numba ten."* After a few more inquiries, I realized she had a bad headache. I went back to my cubicle hoping I had some aspirin but all I had in the way of a pain reliever was Alka-Seltzer.

Bá Klaum watched with uncertainty as I filled a glass half full of water and plunked in two tablets which immediately began to fizz. Her eyes opened wide and she backed away from my bubbling concoction. She had never seen an Alka-Seltzer before and didn't want anything to do with it. I tried to convince her it was medicine – I even sipped a swallow to show her it was okay to drink. But to no avail… she was fearful of my "home brew."

★★★★★

Thanksgiving was like any other Thursday except for a really special meal at the chow hall – turkey and dressing with all the fixings, including pumpkin pie! This written message from the Base Commander was given to each person as they entered the chow hall:

> *"The necessity for keeping the defense of a nation, and the free world, strong and alert has placed you a long way from home on a holiday that is traditionally a family affair. Your family, along with millions of other Americans, thank God this day that you protect our country. Traditionally, Thanksgiving stands for neighborhood churches, friends and family, the smell of fall in the air, your favorite college football game, and turkey and pumpkin pie. But it also stands for much more… a nation founded on the*

principles of a hard won freedom, a nation of plenty with opportunities for all. We thank God this Thanksgiving that there have been in the past and that there are those now willing to risk all that they hold dear that it might remain so. Thanksgiving is an American holiday and you are celebrating it here at Nha Trang Air Force Base Republic of South Vietnam in the finest possible way."

My mind conjured up precious memories of past Thanksgivings – the scrumptious aromas that filled the house, the succulent meal, watching the seasonal festivities on television, and of course, all the football games following the dinner. There's just no substitute for those traditions… and I yearned for them dearly.

My feelings about Thanksgiving were contrary to some servicemen in Vietnam who proclaimed they had nothing for which to be thankful. Granted, a war zone wasn't the most desirable place to be and being separated from family and friends was an additional strain, but despite these burdens, I found a multitude of blessings for which I was thankful. Residing at a secure airbase instead of a ground-pounder in some rice patty was among the top of my list.

★★★★★

A package arrived from Barbara in late November and in it was

my very own Christmas tree complete with lights and decorations! The artificial tree stood no more than thirty inches high and fit perfectly on a shelf in my cubicle. The package also included a gold-painted Styrofoam star made by Barbara's Dad. The tree and colored lights definitely added a touch of Christmas to our otherwise drab barracks.

There were also two stuffed Christmas stockings in the package – one for my roommate and one for me. Barbara sent Richard a stocking so he wouldn't tease me about mine. Like "good little boys," we would wait until Christmas Day to open our stockings. She even personalized each stocking with our names spelled in red glitter, and we proudly hung them next to the Christmas tree.

Our barracks chief reluctantly approved of our colorfully decorated area with the understanding that the tree would be turned off when unattended and that all of the lights would be extinguished if we came under attack.

*****

The much-anticipated Hollywood movie *The Green Berets* made

its debut in Nha Trang at a very appropriate location – the 5th Special Forces Green Beret Camp. Their "theater" was actually a cramped room with about forty folding chairs, a screen, and a projector. The theater was filled to capacity on the first night's showing.

Carl Frost and I hiked over to the camp on the third night hoping to get a seat for the movie. Being early, we easily got in and the place was soon packed with authentic Green Berets. Shortly after the movie began, most of the GIs became disgusted and were shouting back at the screen about the absurdities of the movie. One Green Beret explained, _"This is pure bullshit!"_ and stomped out of the area.

The action film was about some Green Berets, led by John Wayne, trying to persuade a liberal journalist that the war was a good thing for Vietnam and for America. The _Green Berets_ was heavily criticized by movie critics for its over-patriotic and romantic depiction of American involvement in the Vietnam War. After some expected heroism, the film's themes, message, and content suggested the United States would stop the spread of communist insurgencies in the rest of the world by fighting Vietnamese communists in Indochina.

Even to an untrained eye, many factual errors were obvious – pine trees in Vietnam (many outdoor scenes were filmed in Georgia), Claymore mines facing in the wrong direction, soldiers with plastic M-16 rifles, and perhaps the biggest blooper was at the end of the movie which depicted a sunset over the South China Sea. Vietnam's entire coastline faces east, which could never have a sunset!

It was an interesting experience that led me to acquire a cynical view toward Hollywood filmmaking. Thousands of moviegoers in the states got a distorted and inaccurate conception of how the conflict was really being handled.

✱✱✱✱✱

The "snack bar" was a popular place on the airbase where items such as hot dogs, hamburgers, potato chips, and lemonade could be purchased. It was located just around the corner from the chow hall and was one of the few places on base that had ice available. The place was light, airy, and always had floor fans running to cool the area. It was a good place to take a break and enjoy a cold drink. Instead of eating at the chow hall, sometimes I  opted to buy food at the snack bar. A trendy thing there was the jukebox – GIs bought nickel tokens at the counter to play their favorite songs. From the twenty record selection, two songs were played almost continually – *"Kiss Me Goodbye"* sung by Petula Clark and *"We've Got to Get Out of This Place"* performed by *The Animals*.

★★★★★

An extensive and costly installation of a base-wide public address system was completed in October. The new system used  loudspeaker clusters mounted high atop wooden utility poles throughout the base. The primary purpose of the new system was to alert personnel of any impending hostile action or to announce an "all-clear" signal following an attack. Before that system was installed, Security Police drove through the base with a powered megaphone, or a "PsyOps[1]" O2-B aircraft flew overhead using its powerful aerial loudspeakers.

---

[1] *"PsyOps"* (Psychological Operations) aircraft dropped information leaflets and broadcasting messages over the region.

Another use of the PA system was to broadcast a recorded bugle call of *"To the Colors"* when the American flag at headquarters was raised in the morning and *"Retreat"* when the flag was lowered in the late afternoon. Many GIs made a point not to be outside during these times, because if you were, you were expected to stop your activity, face the colors, and salute while the bugle call was playing.

*****

Nha Trang had the dubious distinction as an airbase in South Vietnam with one of the highest rates of venereal disease (VD) among U.S. servicemen. That was due to the fact that the town of Nha Trang was not a restricted access – it was wide open to all sorts of activities. Obviously, a good number of GIs took advantage of that privilege.

To combat that infamous notoriety, our squadron initiated a program to lessen the cases of VD among its members – a dispenser of complimentary condoms was installed adjacent to the mail pick-up window. There was an inconsistency here – many servicemen would receive a letter from their wife or sweetheart back home, and then pick up a handful of condoms all in a single visit to the pick-up window.

My moral principles went against that type of promiscuous activity and I didn't mind the "straight laced" reputation I acquired. I felt a moral obligation to my wife and to God not to indulge in any adulterous acts. Imagine my shock and disbelief when I began having symptoms of gonorrhea!

I reported to Sick Call[1] at 0700 hours and was prescreened by a corpsman. When he heard my symptoms, he told me to return at 0900 hours. I asked, *"Why then?"* He replied, *"That's the time we see all the VD cases."* My heart sank. My mind raced with all sorts of questions – the first and foremost was, *"How could this be possible?"*

I returned at 0900 to find a line of GIs had already formed. I took my place at the end of the line and tried to be inconspicuous. One of the soldiers in line recognized me. He laughed and spoke in a boisterous manner, *"Well now, look who we have here… has your halo gotten a little tarnished?"* I didn't reply to his put-down. I wanted to cover my head with a paper sack.

I finally saw a physician and he asked for the specific date of my most recent sexual contact. He thought I was being contemptuous when I said six months ago during my honeymoon. He said, *"Yeah right… now really, when was it. I can't treat you unless I have this type of information."* I repeated my answer and watched him roll his eyes. *"Okay, we'll first run some tests and then work out a treatment plan."* The physician left and a corpsman then took a blood and urine sample. I was instructed to return the next morning at 0900 hours (not again!) for the results of the tests.

I returned to Sick Call the next morning and saw the same physician from the previous day. He looked over my chart and said he had some good news and some bad news. The good news was I didn't have a venereal disease (I could have told him that!). The bad news was I did have a kidney inflammation, which could produce symptoms much like that of gonorrhea. After a few treatments[2], the

---

[1] Sick Call is a daily lineup of military personnel requiring medical attention.
[2] The treatment was antibiotics and hydrating my system by drinking a liter of water per day under supervision.

condition cleared and the symptoms vanished. My "halo" had survived the ordeal and my reputation remained intact.

★★★★★

I was alone in the armament shop one afternoon checking a launcher when I heard a distant rumble that sounded similar to an in-coming 82mm mortar. I shrugged it off knowing the VC never attacked during broad daylight. Then I heard another – a lot closer. I wondered what was making the sound – surely it wasn't a mortar attack. A third deafening detonation just outside the shop pelted the metal siding of the building with shrapnel. I couldn't believe it – we were being attacked with mortars in the middle of the day!

No sooner than the third round hit, the new base loudspeakers began to wail out an alarm. Because mortar attacks usually occur at night, many senior NCOs who resided off base had never experienced an attack and were in a near panic. Intuitively, I hit the floor and crawled under the workbench and behind a row of metal toolboxes wishing I had my steel helmet and flak vest. I hunkered down and listened intently for additional rounds while whispering a prayer. I dared not run to a bunker because that would make me even more vulnerable.

The range of a Soviet 82mm mortar was about 2½ miles so our attackers were at least that close to the airbase – which was pretty brainless in the daytime taking into account our defenses present. Considering the odds, it was almost a suicidal act. I heard gunfire in the distant and presumed some sort of engagement had taken place.

After about twenty minutes and only three in-coming rounds, the loudspeakers went silent followed by the all-clear signal. We went outside to find a crater pit in the ground about fifty yards from the shop and indentures in the side of the building. The general consensus was that the mortars were launched by the VC as their version of H&I fire.

I never dreamed that would happen – I'd always felt reasonably protected in the daytime. But that incident drove home a point – I couldn't let my guard down for one second regardless of the time of day or night. It was a good lesson – don't take things for granted. Just when I thought a situation was predictable, along came the exception that changed everything.

★★★★★

I received an unexpected package in the mail from my parents and had no idea what could be in the box. I hurried back to the armament shop and opened the box to find two things that I had casually mentioned in one of my letters to Mom and Dad – my sheet music and a small electric window fan! A fan was a premium commodity in Vietnam and those who had one were considered fortunate. My sheet music was a real treasure, and I could hardly wait to play the Chapel's organ again.

I took my fan to the barracks and placed it on a shelf at the head of my bunk. I then pulled away the mosquito netting that surrounded my bunk, because the breeze from the fan would now repel those pesky nuisances. I turned the fan on "high" and climbed in the bunk to give it a try – it was *wonderful* even though it was blowing hot air from the outside. Now if only the power remained on throughout the night, I'd have it made. I had definitely gained an appreciation for some of the simpler things in life!

✳✳✳✳✳

The USO offered a program for any interested servicemen to make a brief thirty-second voice recording to be played over a hometown radio station as a Christmas greeting. A typical greeting would include the identity of the serviceman and a personal message to family members or friends.

I thought a radio greeting would be a nice surprise to Barbara so I recorded a message to her and also mentioned Mom and Dad. I requested my seasonal greeting be broadcast over WSB (AM 750) radio in Atlanta, and I told Barbara in my next letter to be listening to that radio station for a surprise. She listened intently for weeks at home, in the car, and at her work for her "surprise." She never heard it because the message was never played over any radio station – instead, the tape was mailed to Barbara and she received it a few days after Christmas.

✳✳✳✳✳

Another choice amenity at Nha Trang, and something I never expected, was Armed Forces Radio and Television Network that transmitted from Hon Tre Island. The radio programs were available in AM featuring current tunes and news[1] and FM with a more classical format. Barbara sent me an AM/FM radio, which I really appreciated and I listened to traditional music on FM most of the time.

Every night immediately before the sign-off at midnight – they played *Clare de Lune* followed by the *Star Spangled Banner*. Sometimes

---

[1]   In the 1987 film *Good Morning, Vietnam*, actor Robin Williams portrayed an Armed Forces Radio Service (AFRS) disc jockey.

I would tune the dial and listen to distant Vietnamese stations. The music was really strange – a scale of five notes and two semi-notes were used and the classical instruments were various stringed instruments, drums, and gongs.

The television programs were in black-and-white and featured reruns of stateside TV shows; however, there were no commercials which most GIs longed to see! Viewing advertisements would provoke recollections of past times away from Vietnam. The picture was usually fuzzy and required constant fiddling of the TV's "rabbit ears." The squadron's Day Room had a small TV and we'd often crowd into the area on Thursday night to watch *Star Trek*, by far the most popular show of that time.

★★★★★

A rare snowfall blanketed Atlanta on Veteran's Day in mid November and Barbara mailed some photos of the winter scenes. Looking at the pictures made me realize there was yet another thing that I had been denied – *seasons!* In the tropics, it was perpetual summertime – something I once wished for as a youngster.

One of Barbara's photos showed her footprints in the snow to the curbside mailbox to check for any letters. Another was Barbara about to toss a small snowball toward the camera. I showed the pictures to Bá Klaum and she looked puzzled  at the snow. I couldn't make her understand it was frozen water that fell from the sky – a concept totally foreign to anyone who spent his or her whole life near the equator.

I went to the barrack's old refrigerator and scraped some ice into my hand from the freezer compartment. I patted the ice into a small ball and showed Bá Klaum. I then pointed to the snowball in the photo and said, *"Same same."* She looked at me skeptically as if she knew I was trying to fool her and, to my utter astonishment, remarked, *"GI boo coup bullsit!"* I doubled over in laughter because I had never heard her say anything like that before. When I regained my composure, I replied, *"No, no...GI no bullsit!"* I never did convince her frozen water actually could fall from the sky.

★★★★★

I was returning from the flightline one morning and knew something wasn't right when Sgt. Baker met me half way. He said that I needed to report to the Orderly Room immediately. He wouldn't elaborate why my appearance was necessary... just that I needed to get there ASAP. He was dead serious which heightened my anxiety. My first thought was something terribly bad had happened back home and the Red Cross was there to break the news to me. I handed Sgt. Baker my tool pouch and I literally sprinted to the Orderly Room with a wrenching feel of despair in my gut.

Out of breath, I knocked on the door and it was opened immediately by the First Sergeant. He told me to enter and I did – noticing three other people in the room, two being military officers from the Security Police. I was relieved that no one from the Red Cross was there. My mind was in a tailspin trying to make sense of the moment.

One of the officers said, *"Have a seat, Airman, and then tell me what you know about IFFV Headquarters."* What? I knew the IFFV was the Army's First Field Force Vietnam that was headquartered downtown, but that was the extent of my knowledge about that subject. I told the officer what I knew, which was very little. I was really intimidated and desperately wanted to know why I was being interrogated; however, I was overly relieved that it wasn't bad news from home.

"You work with explosive ordinance...right?" he asked. *"Yes sir, I'm a weapons mechanic,"* I replied. He scribbled something on a notepad and then asked, *"Were you off duty last night?"* I replied, *"No sir, I worked the late shift until around midnight."* He again wrote something in his notepad.

After some more baffling questions, he finally disclosed the reason for the interrogation – an explosive charge was found near the IFFV Headquarters the night before and it was set to detonate using an alarm clock inscribed with my name. *My stolen clock was being used to detonate a time bomb!*

I explained in great detail how my clock was stolen during the rescreening project, and I had filed a report with the Security Police. The officer made a phone call and informed me that my report was still on file. That report apparently vindicated me because I was dismissed to return to duty. Before leaving, the officer ordered me to remain silent about the incident[1].

It was a tormenting and harrowing experience. Had I not reported my clock stolen, I would be the prime suspect and most likely indicted. But one question lingered with me – did the interrogating officer really think I was that stupid not to scratch out my name on the clock if I, in fact, planned to bomb IFFV?

---

[1] It was years before I mentioned that incident to anyone, even to Barbara.

★★★★★

I noticed an odd thing about some Vietnamese people – their teeth and gums had a reddish appearance… almost like they were stained. I discovered the staining was due to a type of nut that was chewed to achieve a stimulating, mildly intoxicating effect on the mind much like nicotine.

The highly addictive seed was more commonly known as betel nut, the seed of the betel palm that grows throughout Asia. Betel chewing was a part of many Asian cultures, and preparation techniques varied from region to region. The nut is slivered or grated, often flavored with spices, according to local tradition, and usually wrapped in a betel leaf along with some lime to better extract the intoxicants. Some people also chewed tobacco with betel nut.

After about twenty minutes of chewing, the fibrous residue that remained from the nut was usually spat on the ground, where it stayed visible due to its characteristic bright red color. The red stained ground was a sure indication of the popularity of betel chewing in any area. Strangely enough, betel nut had been found to prevent tooth decay, and some tooth powders contain extracts of betel nut for that reason.

★★★★★

I found that many servicemen were communicating with their families back home using tape recorders instead of written letters. When the BX began stocking the small reel-to-reel recorders, they sold off the shelves like hotcakes. I managed to snag the last one and hoped Barbara could find a compatible recorder. She bought one, and we began to swap tapes on a regular basis. It was a real joy to clearly hear my bride's sweet voice.

We didn't altogether abandon letters because sometimes it was difficult finding a private moment in which to record or play back a tape. One drawback with using tapes was that often we would record over an old tape losing forever the original message. To prevent this from occurring, we began using a fresh tape each time we made a recording.

On one of my early tapes, the sound of an actual mortar attack was captured – I let the recorder run while I took cover on the floor. When I played it back, I decided it was best not to send it to Barbara because the sounds of the mortar detonations, sirens, and overall clamoring of the situation would cause her undue stress. It sounded much worse than it actually was... or was I getting so accustomed to this occurrence that it was becoming commonplace?

★★★★★

When Atlanta came off Daylight Savings Time in late October, Atlanta was exactly twelve hours behind Vietnam. Oftentimes during the evening hours I would wonder what Barbara was doing at that precise moment to begin the day that I had just finished. In a weird way, I felt a connection with her that created a serenity and peace of mind.

When I was in Colorado, Barbara and I would often create a bond by looking at the moon together while speaking to each other over the telephone. Unfortunately, that was impossible now with me on the other side of the world from her. I continued to miss her in the worst way and sought all options to connect with her in any possible manner.

Chapter 10

"...If Only In My Dreams"

December 1968 – February 1969

*"Ability is what you're capable of doing.
Motivation determines what you do. Attitude
determines how well you do it."*

Lou Holtz

In the News...

* *Entertainer Bob Hope and his entourage of celebrities departed for his annual USO tour in early December. Included in this year's show are Ann Margret, Linda Bennett, The Golddiggers, Dick Albers, Penelope Plummer, Rosey Grier, Les Brown, The Honey, Roger Smith, and Elaine Dunn. Their itinerary includes Japan, Korea, Okinawa, Thailand, Guam, and Vietnam.*

* *The Hong Kong influenza pandemic reached its peak the United States in late December with an estimated 50 million infected and an estimated 34,000 deaths. As the name suggests, the virus was first identified in Hong Kong early in 1968 before it spread to the United States, most likely by returning Vietnam War troops. The flu's symptoms include high fever, muscle aches, fatigue, and possibly death.*

* *The top tunes of 1968 saw the Beatle's* "Hey Jude" *top out the billboard ratings followed by* "Young Girl" *by Gary Puckett and the Union Gap,* "People Got to Be Free" *by The Rascals,* "Mrs. Robinson" *by Simon and Garfunkel, and* "Love is Blue" *by Paul Mauriat. With an unexpected social interest in astrology, The Fifth Dimension capitalized on*

141

the trend by recording "Aquarius" which went to the top of the charts in January.

* South Vietnam's Vice-President Nguyen Cao Ky arrived in Paris to lead his country's negotiating team in the expanded peace talks. The Peace talks were deadlocked by a dispute over trivial protocol issues, one of which was the shape of the negotiating table.

* On Christmas Eve, during first manned mission to orbit the moon, Apollo 8 astronauts made a historic live broadcast to Earth. The broadcast included a scripture reading from the book of Genesis that enraged atheist groups across the country.

* In January, explosions aboard the nuclear-powered aircraft carrier USS Enterprise killed 27 sailors and injured 85. The mishap occurred off the coast of Hawaii and was most likely caused by an aircraft rocket on the flight deck. The $6 million damage to the ship was repaired and it returned to action by March.

* Superbowl III was a decisive win for the New York Jets when they defeated the Baltimore Colts at the Orange Bowl in Miami by a score of 16-7. After boldly guaranteeing a victory prior to the game, Jets quarterback Joe Namath completed 17 out of 28 passes for 206 yards, and was named the Super Bowl's Most Valuable Player.

* Republican Richard M. Nixon was sworn into office as the 37th U.S. President by Chief Justice Earl Warren at ceremonies on the east plaza of the Capitol. After the ceremony and inaugural address, 10,000 people attended the inaugural parade. Roughly 2,000 were demonstrators who pelted Nixon's procession with rocks, beer cans, and ink-filled balloons. Once in office, he proposed the Nixon Doctrine, a strategy of replacing American troops with the Vietnamese troops, also called "Vietnamization."

* The U.S. casualty in Vietnam for 1968 surpassed 16,000.

As Christmastime approached, I began to play seasonal music on the Chapel's organ. I had to admit it was odd hearing *Winter Wonderland, Frosty the Snowman,* and *White Christmas* being played with temperatures in the 80's. Mom had mailed my Christmas sheet music, and I continued to enjoy playing the songs I once performed at the restaurant in Atlanta. Capt. Schuermann remarked the tunes made him feel cooler and told me to continue playing seasonal melodies.

While playing the familiar music, my mind would often return for a brief moment to that placid time at home with my parents and new bride. I never embraced the anti-cultural and war protest songs of that turbulent era and, to some individuals of my generation, I was looked upon as being square and geekish – that didn't bother me in the least.

✶✶✶✶✶

In early December, a notice was sent to all work centers in the squadron authorizing the NCOIC to release as many GIs as possible to attend the USO show. It would be in Cam Ranh later in the month – the exact date wasn't specified because such information would be of interest to the enemy. A huge gathering of servicemen would make an opportune target, and a single mortar could inflict mass casualties.

Sgt. Baker polled his personnel and to my surprise, I was the only one to express interest. For many years I had watched film clips from Bob Hope's Christmas show where he entertained thousands of servicemen. I never dreamed one day I'd be one of them.

The specific date of the show was quietly announced (December 22), and about a dozen GIs from Nha Trang would attend the show. I thought surely we'd catch a daily cargo flight to Cam Ranh. I was wrong – the plan was for the group to travel in a vehicle, a piece of news that created some worry for me. I'd much rather be in an airplane over the ocean for a few minutes than in a truck on the ground for an hour. I figured anything was worth seeing Ann Margret... uh, I mean Bob Hope.

The day finally arrived and we all crammed into a 2 ½ ton *"Deuce and a Half"* truck that contained bench seats in the back covered by a canvas top. We departed the security of the airbase and traveled through town to a well-traveled gravel road, which later intersected with the main roadway south to Cam Ranh. The route ran through a valley between two mountains, well away from the shoreline. The truck driver assured us he'd driven the route many times which somewhat eased my worry. After a while, we were really in the boonies with rice paddies on both sides of the road. Despite the monsoon rains, the roadway was reasonably dry and our travel wasn't hampered.

Our trip turned out to be more momentous than expected – as we traveled the rural countryside shortly after our departure, someone asked the question *"Is anyone in the truck armed?"* We looked at each other and every person shrugged their shoulders while shaking their heads. All we had were cameras and lots of film. Someone tapped the glass to the truck's cab and asked the same question. *"No, I thought you guys brought sidearms!"*

There we were – a truckload of American servicemen in a war zone, miles from any U.S. facility, with not even a pocketknife for protection. We could have been commandeered by anyone with a _slingshot!_ I guess all we had on our minds was Ann Margret... uh, I mean Bob Hope.

Despite our lack of preparation, we made the trip without incident. We arrived at Cam Ranh in early afternoon and made our way to the Robert Pugh Memorial Amphitheater. The area was a gently sloping hillside with a permanent stage constructed at the lowest point. I was surprised to see hundreds of servicemen already there – and the show wouldn't start for another six hours! Fortunately, the sky was overcast and the temperature was tolerable. A public address system repeatedly blared the same record album – _Holiday Sing-along with Mitch Miller._ If I hear _"Must be Santa"_ ever again, it'll be much too soon!

Patients from the 6th Convalescent Hospital, identified by blue colored shirts, occupied the area a dozen rows deep directly in front of the stage. Their section was cordoned off by a rope to separate the patients from the other GIs. People on the hillside were mingling about and constantly changing positions, so I took advantage of that by gradually making my way closer to the stage. After a while, I finally reached the rope that sectioned off the hospital patients. I found a blue hospital shirt on the ground and claimed it as my own. I took off my fatigue shirt, inconspicuously slipped on the blue shirt, and crossed under the rope. I had no idea whose shirt I had or worse yet, what kind of injury or disease might have afflicted its owner. At the time I figured anything was worth being close to Ann Margret.

When the show began at 2000 hours, the area was packed with literally thousands of GIs and when Bob Hope came on stage with his trademark golf club and boonie hat, the crowd roared with exuberant cheers. His opening remark was, _"I planned to spend_

Christmas in the States…but I couldn't stand the violence." GIs laughed as he did a stand-up comic routine that had a local flavor. After a few songs by other celebrities, Ann Margret made her first appearance. The crowd erupted with wild cheers and whistles with good reason – she strutted on stage wearing high heels and a dainty negligee. Guys near the stage were privileged to get a whiff of her alluring perfume. To any GI who hadn't seen or smelled a live gorgeous woman in months… that was a serious sensory overload!

The show continued for well over an hour and most entertainers made at least one wardrobe change. The sound of  thunder was heard several times and the clouds finally burst open with a heavy downpour, but the show was not interrupted as the performers and live band continued the entertainment. Ann Margret still looked great even with wet hair (and wet clothes!).

At the close of the show with the rain still pouring, all the cast members joined Bob Hope in singing *Silent Night* as thousands of servicemen joined in – a very moving moment for me. It had been a great time and well worth the hassle. I discarded the wet hospital shirt with the mindset that the benefit was well worth the risk.

Afterwards, as the rain continued to pour, the throngs of soaked GIs scurried to leave the area. Instead of following the roadway out of the arena, a few other GIs and I decided to take a shortcut down a hillside to where the truck was parked. We began our descent slowly at first, but encountered some slippery conditions, which unintentionally sped up our pace. Also, the hillside was much steeper than we anticipated, so basically we were running downhill in the rain....at night. Stupid me, I was in the lead.

Then it happened – I was clotheslined in the neck and thrown violently backwards to the muddy ground. My first thought was I had triggered some sort of booby trap but those devices were almost always fatal... and I most certainly wasn't dead yet. I managed to sit up to regain my senses and assess my injuries – my neck was burning and, for some odd reason, both my hands were throbbing – right in the middle of each palm. There was also a fair amount of blood mixed with the rain and mud. I glanced up through the raindrops and could barely make out what I hit – it was a single strand of barbwire strung across the hillside about five feet off the ground. Fortunately, the other guys following me saw my mishap and stopped before reaching the wire. They came to my assistance right away.

We made it down the hillside to a latrine facility where I further surveyed my injuries in a mirror. My neck was reddened, as expected, but no broken skin – I had hit the wire *between* two razor-sharp barbs! My hands weren't as lucky – when I hit the wire, I instinctively reached up with both hands and grabbed the barbwire piercing both palms, resulting in a bloody puncture in each hand.

It was at that moment I was overwhelmed with what best could be described as a profound religious experience. I had an assuring premonition that a Guardian Angel had been watching over and protecting me. Had I been *two inches* right or left, I could have been fatally pierced in my neck by a barb! The fact that both my palms were punctured symbolized to me God's Son who was nailed to a cross on my behalf. The incident solidified my belief in Divine intervention.

I was thoroughly soaked from the rain, and now I began to shiver due to the traumatic shock from the mishap. I had to get out of those wet clothes. I looked around in the latrine and found an apparently abandoned set of dry Army fatigues...and they were my size! I had no idea why anyone would toss away perfectly dry clothes during a monsoon downpour, but in no time I had a new identity – Army Staff Sergeant Dabney. Then a thought occurred to me that made me shudder – maybe that Dabney guy was in the showers! If so, he'd be out soon and find his clothes missing... and me wearing them! It was time to leave.

Our entire group finally returned to the truck, but I was already aboard lurking in the dark shadows hoping I'd never meet anyone named Dabney. We stopped by the security police headquarters to inquire about obtaining sidearms for our return trip to Nha Trang in the morning. The sergeant on duty asked, *"You're telling me you guys traveled from Nha Trang in that deuce-and-a-half and nobody had a weapon? That was pretty stupid, ya know."* We asked him not to remind us. He said we'd have to individually sign for an M-16 rifle and then turn it in at Nha Trang the next day. When it came time for me to sign the hand receipt, the signature was that of a Sgt. Dabney and I had to create a fictitious service number for my new identity.

After a quick overnight stay, the rain ended and we made our way back to Nha Trang via the same road, but it had become muddy due to the previous night's downpour. The return trip was far less anxious because we all were well armed – a drastic contrast to the trip the day before. After returning to the airbase, I immediately discarded the "borrowed" fatigues and breathed a sigh of relief. Despite all the stupid things that I did, it was an experience not soon to be forgotten.

*****

The 21st TASS was scheduled to add another type of aircraft to its inventory – the OV-10 *Bronco*. It was a turboprop light attack and observation aircraft built by North American Rockwell. In preparation for the OV-10's arrival in March 1969, I received orders to go TDY (temporary duty) to Detach-  ment 1, 504 Tactical Air Support Group, located at Phan Rang Airbase for aircraft familiarization. Phan Rang Airbase was a coastal facility about 50 miles south of Nha Trang where new FAC pilots would undergo their in-country checkout before being assigned to a TASS unit. Phan Rang was unofficially called the Forward Air Control University or better known as FAC U.

I wasn't too keen on the TDY assignment. I became really annoyed to discover my mail would not be forwarded from Nha Trang during the TDY. Another concern was that the TDY might have an impact on my R&R to Hawaii scheduled in mid-January. I was relieved when my TDY orders stated, *"Not to exceed 30 calendar days,"* which was well before my R&R date.

On December 3, I packed my duffle bag and reported to the passenger terminal. Anytime a serviceman traveled in-country, his personal protection and weapon went with him, so I wore my helmet and flak vest with my M-16 rifle slung over my shoulder. I boarded a C-123 cargo transport aircraft for the nonstop flight to Phan Rang. A single-striped Airman was on board and he looked scared stiff. That was a déjà vu experience for me because six months ago I was that frightened Airman. I wondered if he perceived me as a scruffy battle veteran. Looks can surely be deceiving!

Upon arrival at the TDY location, I reported to the OV-10 squadron only to find they had no idea why I was there – they hadn't been advised of the aircraft familiarization program they were supposed to conduct. I was pretty aggravated about that SNAFU[1] and talked via telephone with Sgt. Baker. He said to remain at Phan Rang a few days and maybe I could absorb something worthwhile. So I just loitered about the work area asking questions and received not one definitive answer. I felt like I was embarrassing them so I quit asking questions and dug into the Technical Orders. I picked up a few tidbits of information that made some sense. My major source of information was from a pilot in-briefing which I was allowed to attend... but was told to sit in the back of the room and to not say a word.

After a week of that nonsense, I called Sgt. Baker and told him my time had become totally nonproductive and pleaded with him to terminate my TDY. He agreed and informed me that plans had changed – we were not getting the OV-10 after all. When were they going to tell me? The entire scenario had been for naught! I happily made reservations for a flight back to Nha Trang the next morning.

That evening after supper, I visited a Red Cross Center not too far from my barracks. The place was fashioned to resemble a living room with cushy furniture and a coffee table covered with all sorts of reading material. The walls were adorned with travel posters of exotic and alluring destinations. Pinned to a bulletin board were

---

[1] Situation normal – all fouled up!

several letters from stateside school children who wanted to be a pen pal with a serviceman in Vietnam. I randomly pulled off a letter and discovered it was from an eleven year-old girl in Gaston, Indiana named Connie Berry. The letter was introductory in nature without much detail. I had some time to spend so I replied to her letter and told her about myself. My letter was short – just a single page. I addressed an envelope and dropped the letter in the outgoing mail bin.

The next morning, I boarded a C-7 _Caribou_ for the return trip to Nha Trang. Soon after takeoff, the aircraft developed a minor hydraulic leak that required a nonscheduled stop at Cam Ranh Airbase. Gary Howell, the Best Man at my wedding, was stationed in Cam Ranh so I looked him up and we had an enjoyable time together reminiscing over past times. I spent the night on a spare cot in his hootch. The following morning after the hydraulic leak had been repaired, we resumed our flight to Nha Trang.

Once back at my squadron, I discovered the base had been mortared the night before and, unlike previous attacks, the mortars were aimed at the lower flightline where I would have been working. Perhaps a minuscule hydraulic leak had prevented me from being injured or even worse – killed. I felt like that wasn't a coincidence but rather my Guardian Angel doing another fine job of protecting me.

✸✸✸✸

Two weeks later, I received a letter from my pen pal in Indiana. Connie seemed thrilled that I answered her letter – the only one in her class of twenty-five students to receive a reply. She read my letter aloud to her class and the whole group "adopted" me as their class pen pal. Connie included a photograph of herself – a delightful looking young girl with long dark hair[1]. I wrote to her

with a little more detail of myself. I received an immediate reply from the class wanting to know more about my daily routine.

We exchanged about five letters and I suppose the novelty wore off after a while. Eventually, we lost touch but I saved all her letters hoping one day I might have the opportunity to meet her. Unfortunately, that never happened.

✳✳✳✳✳

On Christmas Eve, our barracks had an impromptu celebration that turned a bit over-zealous. I wanted Barbara to share in our festivities so I brought out my tape recorder and captured light-hearted laughter, innuendos about sexy girls being present, a few irreverent Christmas carols and overall silliness. It sounded like we were all smashed, but not a drop of alcohol had been consumed – we were just having some fun to vent our discontent about being where we were at that particular time.

Meanwhile back in Atlanta, unbeknownst to me, Barbara had been bedridden for a week with the Hong Kong flu – a very contagious influenza that had reached a pandemic in the States. She had made no mention in her daily letters that she was ill – she didn't want me to worry and later I half-heartedly admonished her for not telling me. She did tell me when she played the tape of our

---

[1] As of this writing, Connie is now 52 years of age. Attempts to locate her have been futile.

Christmas party, it lifted her spirits, made her feel better, and put a smile on her face. I had no idea my tape would have such therapeutic value.

*****

Little did I know on that Christmas Eve, a drama was unfolding that had most people in the world glued to a television – a manned U.S. Apollo spacecraft with three astronauts aboard orbiting the moon for the very first time. I had been an avid and passionate follower of the space program ever since the entire student body of my high school assembled in the auditorium on a Friday morning to watch a blurry picture on a small black and white television. History was being made as astronaut Alan Shepard made the first sub-orbital flight in Freedom 7 on May 5, 1961.

Unlike many guys in that era who idolized sports figures, my heroes became a group of brave men called astronauts who exhibited raw courage by riding rockets into space, especially when unmanned predecessor rockets had unexpectedly exploded violently on the launching pad.

I was distressed that I was unable to follow NASA's race to the moon with the Soviet Union. I knew an actual moon landing was imminent and hoped it would take place after my DEROS so I could witness it firsthand[1].

---

[1] Despite the decade's turmoil, efforts to achieve JFK's goal to send men to the moon before 1970 was virtually insulated from the Vietnam War and domestic unrest. Fortunately, the public's support for the lunar program remained high. Apollo was a bright glow of promise in that dark and anxious era. Apollo 11 landed on the moon on July 20, 1969, fifty-nine days after I returned from Vietnam.

★★★★★

We finished our work early on Christmas Day and Sgt. Baker granted everyone liberty starting at noon. I returned to the barracks to have my personal Christmas time alone – that was the second consecutive Christmas I spent away from family. Sitting there on my bunk on Christmas Day in a place so far removed from my loved ones was excruciating. Christmas season was dear to me because of all the happy times spent with family – most all my aunts, uncles, and cousins would congregate at our home on Christmas night to visit with my aging grandmother "Granny Rice," who lived with us. Being removed from those family times was almost unbearable. The lyrics of the Christmas song *"I'll be Home for Christmas"* took on a special meaning for me – especially the ending verse, *"...if only in my dreams."*

I opened my presents from Barbara and found a wonderful scrapbook of all our times together starting with our first date. The book contained ticket stubs, programs, souvenirs, photographs, and mementos from the past three years – I loved it! It was so special because it was a labor of love that could not be purchased anywhere. I got some more gifts but none as special as my scrapbook.

My roommate arrived and together we opened our Christmas stockings. Barbara had packed them full of silly juvenile items such as yoyos, Slinkys, Frisbees, chewing gum and Kool-aid mix. I was so thankful Barbara included Richard in that Christmas tradition because, sadly, his stocking was his only Christmas present.

On the spur of the moment, Richard and I decided to go to the beach – we wanted to create a memory of swimming on Christmas Day. We took along some of our new toys and tossed around a

Frisbee until I missed a catch and the disc sailed into the ocean, never to be seen again.

Christmas dinner was served that evening at the chow hall and just like the meal at Thanksgiving, it was a lavish and delicious feast that I enjoyed immensely. There was a long wait in the chow line and the place was packed with GIs, but the meal was well worth the wait. Some of the entrée selections were actually fresh including milk and fruit. Included in the menu handout was this message to all Armed Forces personnel in Vietnam from General Creighton Abrams:

> *"Christmas has a special meaning for American soldiers in Vietnam. Amid the tragedy and ugliness of war, the Holy Season reminds us of the joy and beauty of peace. In a land whose people struggle for a better life, the Christmas message brings cheer and hope for the future.*
>
> *We who serve in this distant land may be justly proud. On this Christmas Day, no finer gift may one provide than to give of his own that his brother might share what he himself enjoys. This is what we are doing as we assist in supporting the Vietnamese in their struggle to maintain independence.*
>
> *My best wishes to each of you and to your family on this Christmas Day. As we face the coming New Year, may we each pray for success in our mission, peace on Earth, and goodwill for all mankind."*

✸✸✸✸✸

Six days later there was another celebration at our barracks – a New Year's Eve party, and unlike the party at Christmas, the festivity was organized and attended by more people than just those living in our barracks. Colored lights were strung overhead, the water jug was filled with orange juice and Smirnoff, music played over speakers placed outside the barracks, beer was abundant, and steaks were acquired by swapping smoke grenades for beef with our Special Forces comrades during a clandestine rendezvous. Our Squadron Commander and the Base Commander both accepted our invitation and made a brief appearance – a good way to boost morale. Much to our relief, they made no mention or inquiries about where we got all the party food.

Everything was going great and everyone kept an eye on the time. With sixty seconds remaining until the New Year, we all gathered outside for a mass countdown. At the stroke of midnight, we were ready to toast the occasion when our celebration was interrupted by *automatic rifle fire*. Instinctively, everyone fell to the ground spilling drinks and plates of food. Everything got quiet except for the music playing and sound of the gunfire – it was *so close!* Would the VC use the occasion for a ground assault? There was no better time for an attack than during a party when our defenses were relaxed.

It didn't take long to assess the situation – one of our inebriated partygoers had climbed onto the roof of our barracks with his M-16 rifle. At midnight, he emptied a full clip of ammo into the air in full automatic mode thinking he'd add his own noisemaker to the celebration. When the clip was empty, he tried to come down but lost his footing and rolled off the roof, landing unconscious on top of the bunker. One partygoer got up, brushed off the dirt on his uniform, and muttered a profanity about the stupidity of the drunken GI. He retrieved the rifle but walked away from the GI sprawled out in the sandy bunker.

The party resumed and continued well into the morning hours. The catch phrase that evening was *"Welcome 1969"* because that's the year all the people at the party were scheduled to return to the World.

★★★★★

As January arrived, so did my anticipation of going to Hawaii[1] and being with Barbara. I had to have a mandatory medical checkup to make sure I wasn't harboring any tropical illnesses or venereal disease. Any GI testing positive for VD would be denied his R&R – not an area of concern for me.

January 13 finally arrived and I flew to Cam Ranh Airbase to connect with flight P210 to Hawaii. I exchanged all my MPC for U.S. currency – a dollar bill looked so big compared to MPC. It was strange having coins in my pocket which seemed unusually heavy. I was required to have in my possession at least $200 cash for use while on the R&R. The chartered DC-8 aircraft departed on time, re-fueled at Anderson AFB in Guam, and then continued on to Hawaii.

Somewhere the plane crossed the dateline and arrived in Honolulu two hours before we departed Cam Ranh! After claiming our bags, we boarded several Army buses for our twenty-minute ride to the R&R Center at Fort DeRussy, an Army installation located directly on Waikiki Beach. Barbara arrived in Honolulu the previous day so she could meet me at the R&R center.

---

[1] More than half a million servicemen were brought to Hawaii on R&R flights during the Vietnam War, and the financial impact was huge. Spending by the military people, their friends and family who flew to Hawaii to greet them, topped $191 million from August 1966 to early 1973.

I could feel my anxiety mounting as we neared the Fort. Before we were allowed to exit the bus, an Army officer boarded to reiterate the absolute deadline for everyone to be back at Fort DeRussy for the return trip to Vietnam. If anyone failed to show, that person would be considered AWOL[1] and charges would be levied against him. Every GI was given an R&R

> **IMPORTANT**
>
> YOUR DATE OF ARRIVAL IS
>
> 13 JAN 1969
>
> YOU ARE TO REPORT BACK TO THE R&R CENTER, NOT LATER THAN
>
> 2300 HRS / 18 JAN 1969
>
> OR TO THE HONOLULU INTER-NATIONAL AIRPORT NOT
>
> LATER THAN 2400 HRS
>
> 18 JAN 1969
>
> R&R PHONE 5432673

identification card that most Hawaiian merchants would honor with discount pricing, and on the reverse side of the card was the specific date and time for returning to Fort DeRussy. The officer also said that air flights from Hawaii to the U.S. mainland were prohibited for any R&R serviceman.

The bus doors opened and all the servicemen hastily filed out to find wives and loved ones standing in two parallel lines about ten feet apart. We began to walk through the human corridor looking for our family. Happy squeals were heard as women broke rank and rushed to their servicemen. I looked intently for Barbara but the area became congested with lingering couples. I became concerned that she wasn't there – that somehow she missed her flight. My worry vanished when I spotted her – she looked as beautiful as ever with a huge smile on her face and tears in her eyes.

---

[1] During any certain Hawaiian R&R, there was an average of 3% no-shows. Supposedly the AWOL GIs returned to the U.S. mainland as fugitives.

She rushed to me and wrapped her arms around my neck. I felt like I was in a dream – a wonderful and magnificent dream.

The next six days were like a fantasy – H&I cannon fire was replaced by ukulele music; jeeps and armored personnel carriers

were now modern sleek automobiles; brightly colored flowers and clothing replaced olive drab; and I shared a double bed with my wife! We had an incredible experience sight-seeing Honolulu and walking hand-in-hand on Waikiki Beach at sunset. Having fresh food and fruit was a real delight. We stayed at the Hawaiana Hotel within easy walking distance to the beach. I almost had to pinch myself to make sure it was really happening.

I had longed to visit the USS Arizona Memorial at Pearl Harbor but, to my extreme disappointment, the harbor had been placed off limits to the public on the day of my arrival. During a training exercise at sea, a tragic explosion and subsequent fire had occurred aboard the aircraft carrier USS Enterprise[1], and the crippled ship had limped back to Pearl Harbor. All tours to the Arizona Memorial were suspended for an indefinite length of time due to the sensitivity of the incident. What I did see were replica

---

[1] Ironically, 38 years later, our oldest son Scott would serve on the USS Enterprise as a Naval Officer.

World War II vintage aircraft depicting the Japanese attack on Pearl Harbor for a soon to be released motion picture *"Tora! Tora! Tora!"*

High on our agenda was to visit the National Memorial Cemetery located in an extinct volcano on a hillside near Honolulu. The 116-acre memorial, called *"Punch Bowl,"* is the final resting place for over 45,000 Americans killed in World War II. Barbara's uncle is buried there and, to our knowledge, we are the only family members to ever visit or place flowers at his gravesite.

One aspect about being in Hawaii I didn't expect – my body was acclimated to very hot weather and Hawaii wasn't nearly as warm as Vietnam. I stayed chilled most all the time and couldn't walk past knee-deep water in the ocean. Conversely, Barbara came from winter temperatures and thought Hawaii's weather was wonderful!

In fine Hawaiian tradition, we purchased brightly colored matching outfits. That eve-  ning Barbara wore her new muumuu and I wore my matching shirt to see a Polynesian Review and celebrity Don Ho at *Duke Kahanamoku's* nightclub. Don Ho sang his famous *"Tiny Bubbles"* and *"I'll Remember You,"* one of Barbara's favorite songs. At one point in the show, he recognized all the R&R couples in the audience and the crowd responded with standing ovation – a humbling and overwhelming moment for me.

---

¹ At the time of its initial movie release, *Tora Tora Tora* proved to be a major hit in Japanese movie theaters, but a box office flop in U.S. theaters.

The next afternoon while we were finishing lunch at a sidewalk café, a nicely dressed, older gentleman approached and immediately apologized for his interruption. He introduced himself as Mr. Norman Finley from Dayton, Ohio, and he wanted to know if we were an R&R couple. I told him we were and thought for sure he was some kind of a salesman or scam artist. He then explained he had just spent time with his son who had returned to Vietnam the previous day and that he was soon leaving for New Zealand. He said he sincerely appreciated the Armed Forces' sacrifices made for the country and, as a token of his gratitude, wanted us to join him for dinner that night. *What?*

Barbara and I were stunned, not knowing how to respond to such a sudden and unsolicited proposal – this man was a total stranger. Servicemen bound to Hawaii were warned of scoundrels who preyed on unsuspecting R&R couples in Honolulu so my skepticism was high. He then said that if we decided not to accept his offer, he would fully understand our reasons. He wasn't pushy or assertive in any manner. He said he would return to his table and if we decided to be his guest at dinner, come over to discuss the arrangements –otherwise, we could just leave and he'd understand. He again humbly apologized for his interruption and returned to his table and sat down alone with his back toward us.

Barbara and I looked at each other with mounting uncertainty. We exchanged whispers about what just happened and found we were both torn by his true motives and our decision to join him for a meal. At first we felt the smartest thing to do would be to leave without further dealings with this stranger. On the other hand, the man appeared genuine with noble intensions and desired to honor a serviceman and his wife.

After much deliberation, we decided to accept his offer with the condition the restaurant was in a public place and not secluded. Mr. Finley appeared pleased with our acceptance and told us to select the restaurant of our choice. That night we had a delightful free meal at a nice steak house in the heart of Honolulu. Mr. Finley was the perfect host – very polite and gracious. We warmed up to him a bit but were still cautious.

Following the meal, he surprised us again with an invitation to be his guest at one of the many stage shows in Honolulu. I thought to myself, *"Okay, get ready... here it comes!"* I felt surely his true intentions were about to surface which would explain his unusual generosity. But that was not the case. Our choice of entertainment was *"The Tommy Sands Show,"* the featured headliner at the *Outrigger Hotel* and was within easy walking distance from the restaurant. Again, Mr. Finley agreed to anything we wanted and the three of us had an enjoyable evening at the nightclub at his expense.

When we said our good-byes, Mr. Finley thanked us for our companionship and for the acceptance of his invitations. He said the evening had been very special for him and wished us good fortune and blessings. We knew then he was sincere and his intentions were honest. It felt awkward being the recipient of such generosity from a stranger, but in retrospect, we're glad we did, because had we walked away from him at the café, we would have been denied the warmth and kindness of a special gentleman named Mr. Norman Finley. We never heard from him again.

Six days passed much too quickly and it was time for Barbara and I to again part ways. We avoided saying *"Good-Bye"* by replacing it with *"See you in May!"* Things were a lot different from my previous departure – I now had only four months to go and my anxiety level was almost nonexistent. Still, it was so difficult leaving a paradise with my wife and returning to a war. Once back at Nha Trang, I immediately got back into my routine but with the indelible memory of an extraordinary time with my new bride.

✴✴✴✴✴

When I returned from R&R, I found that a few barracks had started a new trend – they adopted various live-animal mascots. Among the critters were monkeys, lizards, birds, and dogs – any type of animal that could be kept in the barracks without too much hassle. These indigenous animals were acquired mostly from our Army comrades who frequently patrolled the jungles beyond the base boundary.

My barracks adopted a young female puppy – no more than six weeks old. Having a pet dog most all my life, I became attached to the animal and cared for it regularly by sneaking food from the chow hall to feed it. The animal was plagued with fleas and when I mentioned it to my parents, they sent me a flea collar. During my duty hours, I kept the dog tethered by a piece of rope between the barracks and the bunker, being mindful to keep its water bowl filled. At night, the puppy slept on the floor in my cubical.

Inevitably, the First Sergeant could no longer tolerate that menagerie of animals and finally proclaimed, *"We ain't running no damn zoo around here. I want all these animals outta here by noon Friday!"* I didn't want to abandon the dog so I decided to give her to Bá Klaum. She had children at home and they'd love to have a pet.

On Thursday, I reluctantly gave the mascot to Bá Klaum and she was overly appreciative of my generous gesture. I felt comfort-

able about that arrangement. A week passed and I asked Bá Klaum about the dog. She replied, *"Dog good!"* That pleased me knowing the dog had a new home. Several weeks passed and again I casually asked about the dog. She looked puzzled and gave the same answer. Then she *rubbed her stomach*!

What!? Does that mean....? Did she eat ...? Was the *"dog good!"* because it was a great pet, or because it was a great meal? Yes, it was true – the ingredients in a soup that she served to her family were vegetables seasoned with dog meat. I never warmed up to the customs of Southeast Asia.

★★★★★

Sgt. Johns' DEROS arrived in early February and he returned to the World. His stateside duty assignment was at Luke AFB in Arizona. I really hated to see Sgt. Johns leave – he was even-tempered and working for him was pleasant. He not only knew how to supervise people, he also knew the technical aspects of our discipline. He was a career NCO and my first supervisor in the Air Force with whom I had great respect.

Even though he denied it, I suspect he was instrumental in my lofty accolades from PACAF. His support and encouragement with my suggestion was the catalyst for many undeserved kudos to come – and for that, I was eternally grateful.

*****

The chalkboard at the Dustbowl Theater announced the nightly movie as *"None but the Brave"* staring Frank Sinatra. For some bizarre reason, movies with a war theme were popular and well attended. As expected, the open-air theater was packed and the movie started on time. The movie was about American and Japanese soldiers, stranded on a Pacific island during World War II, making a temporary truce to survive.

Unbeknownst to the movie patrons, a small faction of Viet Cong commandos was secretly advancing toward our military installation near the far bank of the river. That was incredibly stupid – the Special Forces Camp was between them and us and  the Green Berets out numbered the VC commandos a thousand to one! Sentry guards quickly detected their presence and the ensuing engagement began. A Spooky gunship was scrambled and was over their location immediately. Miniguns spewed their fury as the gunship circled the beleaguered target. Every fifth round of each minigun was a tracer that illuminated its path with a red ball of fire – resembling someone hosing the ground from the air with a Roman candle, only a lot faster.

The moviegoers abandoned the celluloid in favor of the real thing. We turned our undivided attention to the real firefight that was occurring just beyond the airbase so the projectionist shut off the movie. The roar of the miniguns was ominous. No wonder the

Vietnamese dubbed the AC-47 gunship *"Puff the Magic Dragon"* – it roared and spit red fire just like a legendary dragon.

The miniguns went silent and the aircraft returned to the airbase. A cheer rang out from the moviegoers and the crowd dispersed without any desire to see the movie's conclusion. We all knew Frank Sinatra would be victorious… just like Spooky!

★★★★★

For some time I had noticed a construction project underway on the southwest side of the administration building. I was delighted to find the project involved creating a new workspace for our dock maintenance and for some of the other squadron work centers. Our present docks were cramped, crude and makeshift – maintenance workers were forever getting in the way of each other.

Two A-frame metal canopies that were illuminated for night operation covered the new docks. The walls of the docks were actually protective revetments. The work center building was an insulated metal building that housed several shops – each shop being cordoned by wire-wall dividers with a lockable entrance door.

The official opening of the new area included a ceremonious ribbon cutting by the Squadron and Base Commanders while a *Skymaster* was towed into the docks as the commemorative first aircraft to use the new facility. All squadron personnel were in attendance and afterwards, we were all treated to a food and beer bash – much like previous Commander's Calls.

The new docks were immediately put into service and we were ready to abandon the old docks that resembled a junkyard more than a maintenance complex. To add a little color to the otherwise drab décor of the new docks, the sheet metal shop fabricated aluminum "flowers" that were brightly painted and planted in a row next to the administration building. No one would admit it, but that little "extra" made the area more cheerful and pleasant to work around – which inevitably boosted morale and productivity.

★★★★★

Richard Bush entered our cubical with uncharacteristic enthusiasm despite being beet-red with sunburn. *"You just gotta go to the island next time… it was so awesome!"* he exclaimed. I had no earthly idea what he was talking about, so I asked, *"Slow down… what are you trying to say?"* He caught his breath and said more slowly, *"There's this small island that you can walk to… the water is only chest high. A reef is just beyond the island toward the ocean with tons of fish…I've been out there swimming all day. Some buddies of mine from the SOS[1] squadron go there all the time… they asked me to tag along today. I'm telling ya, you gotta go next time…it was great!"*

That was a tempting invitation even though such a venture was totally unauthorized. I weighed the risks and concluded that I'd forever regret not taking the gamble. I told Richard that I'd try to go with him next week when I was on night duty. He was eager to return to the island and the next time he'd take his brand new Nikon camera.

---

[1] Special Operations Squadron

It was all set – two other GIs from the squadron also accepted his invitation and we'd all go the following week. On Monday we caught the downtown bus with an armload of belongings including cameras, towels, flip-flop sandals, and the makings for lunch. No one in our group had any sidearms and, being a bit apprehensive, I secretly included in my stash an Emergency Locator Transmitter (ELT), a sheathed survival knife, and a smoke grenade. I also had the 35mm camera I bought before going to Hawaii.

We exited the bus at a location that wasn't a routine stop and forged on foot through a seaside fishing village – the occupants were friendly and waved to us. The island came into view – a small outcropping of rocks and boulders about fifty yards off shore. Once at the water, we undressed down to our swimsuits but kept on our boots. We rolled our belongings to better carry them above our heads while making the short trek through the water.

We began our walk and quickly found Richard had underestimated the water depth – his previous visit to the island

obviously was made during low tide. Several times the water was chin-deep and once I stepped off a submerged rock and my head went underwater...but I managed to keep my belongings dry. We all made it to the island's rocky shoreline intact. Richard said there was a perfect spot on the seaward side of the island that we could use as a central location. We made our way around the shoreline and found the area he had mentioned. It had some huge rock boulders adjacent to a shallow shoreline which made it an ideal location to stay.

I could hardly wait to get in the water. Richard had somehow acquired a diving mask and snorkel to view the abundant marine life, and we took turns using them. The reef was just as magnificent as I had imagined with all types of brightly colored tropical fish scurrying about. I had never seen anything like that before except in an aquarium. I saw a jellyfish that looked like a parachute with long tentacles. It was translucent and propelled itself with slow rhythmic pulsations of its body. I kept my distance because the long tentacles could deliver a nasty sting – so I was told. A school of bright yellow fish darted by and the sea bottom was teaming with all sorts of coral life. It was all so wonderful.

We swam for most of the morning, and during that time, a fishing boat occupied by two fishermen came near and disappeared behind the island. I assumed they were headed for the village we had seen earlier.

Shortly before noon we came out of the water to have lunch in the shade of the rock boulders. We all snapped a lot of photos of the area – I wished I could have photographed the sea life, which was the real show. Richard's description of the expedition was perfect... it was  an awesome experience and I was glad I decided to make the trip.

Later that afternoon, we returned to the water for one last look before we had to leave – I had duty at 1600 hours and wasn't sure how long it would take to get back to the base. As we collected our things, Richard casually asked, *"Did anyone move my camera... it was right here a while ago."* No one knew anything of the whereabouts of the camera. Then I made a startling discovery – my camera was gone too! Richard went into a frenzy looking everywhere for his very expensive Nikon camera. I began looking too, but the two cameras were nowhere to be found. Apparently, we had a stealth visitor in our midst – most likely a fisherman from the boat – who stole our cameras while we were preoccupied in the water.

Richard became infuriated and angrily exclaimed that he was going to *"whip some ass"* at the fishing village. We had to calm him down and told him to think about our situation – we were away from base, unarmed, at an unauthorized location, outnumbered, outwitted, and sunburned – and he wanted to have a physical altercation with a Vietnamese fisherman in his own village!

We packed up and made our way back to the shore. We told Richard not to even think about doing anything stupid when we walked through the village. He reluctantly restrained himself, and we reached the roadway without incident.

Once back at base, we reported the theft to the Security Police but were less than truthful about where the incident occurred. Richard was inconsolable about the loss of his prize camera – he had aspirations of becoming a professional photographer one day. My camera was far less expensive, and though the theft was unfortunate, my loss was easily recoverable. My biggest regret was losing all the memorable photos of the island.

*****

I received an oversized envelope from Amy Brockman, one of Barbara's high school friends who taught second grade in Topeka, Kansas. Amy had given her class an assignment to write a letter to a serviceman currently serving in Vietnam, so when she got my mailing address from Barbara, Amy sent me thirty-three letters from her students.

The letters were darling and written with the mindset typical of seven year-old children – some more serious than others. Most all the letters included the saying, *"I hope you win the war."* I envied their innocence and was disheartened knowing too soon they would be thrust into reality that would most likely shatter their childish perspectives.

I couldn't reply to each student so I wrote one letter to the whole class thanking them for all the letters. I told them I'd be their pen pal but no student wrote me again.

*****

In late February, my much anticipated orders arrived that informed me of my stateside assignment, which could be anywhere in the continental U.S. I scanned the orders looking intently for the location. It was the 474th Tactical Fighter Wing at Nellis AFB in Nevada. *Nevada?* I had requested a location in Georgia – I realized then why the forecast form[1] was better known as a "dream sheet." I knew about a vast bombing range in the Nevada desert so I assumed I'd be stationed at some remote airfield in a barren region.

---

[1] A "Forecast Form" was used by the Air Force to allow servicemen the opportunity to request his or her next assignment location. If openings were available at the desired base, an assigned would be made.

After some research, I discovered Nellis AFB was near *Las Vegas!* I knew Las Vegas was famous for its casinos, showgirls, and big time entertainers – but I never thought about people actually living there.

I discovered the 474th flew the new and controversial swept-winged F-111 fighter jet. Finally, I'd be working with a high performance aircraft, but I doubted seriously I'd ever have a chance to ride in one like I had with the FACs. I wondered just how long I'd be at Nellis – I would have twenty-eight months remaining in my enlistment when I reported – plenty of time to be reassigned again or, worse yet, pull another Vietnam tour.

I couldn't wait to write to Barbara about the assignment. I wasn't sure how she'd take the news, especially being so far from Atlanta – we were expecting a location somewhere east of the Mississippi River. We didn't want to be assigned too close to home but I thought Nevada was a bit too far.

Barbara was thrilled and couldn't believe the news that we would be living in Las Vegas! Of all the places we could have been stationed, Nellis AFB was the best of locations. Living in Las Vegas was a strange way to begin a marriage… even though we'd have been married over a year by the time we arrived. Las Vegas – what a contrast to Vietnam!

*****

The mamasans in the cantonment area would routinely take turns preparing midday meals for their entire group. The community meal usually occurred during the lull period while the washed clothes dried in the sun. On one particular day, Bá Klaum was preparing some type of leafy vegetable seasoned with a fish sauce. She was cooking the ingredients over an electric hot plate in our barracks' Day Room.

When I entered the barracks, I was met by a strong, pungent smell of rotten fish. As I walked toward the Day Room, the stench got worse. Bá Klaum looked up and acknowledged my presence with a quick nod. I held my nose while pointing to the smelly concoction and said with a nasal whine, *"Numba ten!!"* She chuckled and refuted, *"Nuóc Mám numba one!"* as she continued to stir the putrid mixture.

There's a good reason Nuóc Mám (pronounced *Nook Maum*) had a rotten fish odor – that's exactly what it was. Anchovies were layered in vats containing a salty brine solution for at least one year. The mixture ferments and the potent liquid is drained from the bottom and then poured back in the vat from the top to recycle the process. Nuóc Mám was used as a dipping or cooking sauce much like soy sauce and was the main flavoring in the Vietnamese diet as their main source of salt.

The major problem with preparing Nuóc Mám in the barracks was that everything absorbed that putrid fish odor for days. The stench permeated our clothes, bedding, and bunks. The barracks chief let Bá Klaum know in uncertain terms that Nuóc Mám was not allowed in the barracks.

*****

The Vietnamese New Year was called Tết Nguyên Đán but was more commonly known as simply Tết. It is based on the Chinese calendar which recognizes twelve lunar months instead of one solar year. In 1969, the New Year began on February 17 and ushered in the *"Year of the Earth Rooster."* Mamasans and other Vietnamese employees on base took a three-day holiday during that time.

Tết was the most important and popular Vietnamese holiday. During Tết, people usually return to their families to worship at the family altar or visit the graves of their ancestors. Although Tết was a universal holiday among all Vietnamese, each region and religion had its own customs.

Preparations for Tết started months before the actual celebration. People tried to pay off their debts in advance so they could be debt-free at the beginning of Tết. Parents bought new clothes for their children to wear when Tết arrived. Because a lot of commercial activity would cease during the celebrations, people tried to stock up on supplies as much as possible. In the days leading up to Tết, the streets and markets were full of people – everyone busy buying food, clothes, and decorations for their homes.

Regrettably, during the 1968 Tết holiday on January 31, the Viet Cong and North Vietnamese Army disrupted the otherwise festive occasion with one of the strongest and concerted offenses of the war by simultaneously attacking more than one hundred towns and cities, including Saigon and thirty-six provincial capitals.

For the first time, the battlefield shifted from the jungles and rice patties to the urban city streets. The attack, at the time, was the largest battle of the war. In Nha Trang, the VC used the Buddha statue as a stronghold to assault the airbase and other military installations. The U.S military forces were not allowed to return fire in fear of desecrating the statue.

The attacks took the South Vietnamese and U.S. Forces by total surprise, and the enemy, due to the shock factor, initially made significant strides in the offense[1]. In the end, the VC were eventually forced to retreat due to massive casualties.

As the Lunar New Year approached in 1969, all military forces intensified their security efforts to thwart another enemy offense. The airbase went on permanent Yellow Alert and we waited for any type of repercussion. For whatever reason, there were no significant activities reported that time around.

★★★★★

Bá Klaum asked me to purchase some staple goods because the stores in town had sold out due to the upcoming Tết celebration. I took her list to the exchange and bought what was available, but there was still a problem – she couldn't get the stash off base. Larry Phillips, a friend from the squadron, had previously been to Bá Klaum's home and had access to a jeep, so we loaded the staple items and headed off base.

We arrived at Bá Klaum's home and she insisted we come inside. She lived in a small dirt-floor dwelling that resembled a shack more than a house. It had a low ceiling and Larry, being over six feet tall, had to constantly stoop or otherwise he'd bang his head on the ceiling. There was no electricity, candles were everywhere, and the home was dotted with Catholic artifacts. Bá Klaum offered us a meal but we quickly declined – neither of us could stomach Nuóc Mám.

---

[1]   This was a major turning point of the war because the home front was led to believe by military leaders that the United States was winning the conflict.

Bá Klaum was married and had five children, the oldest not yet twelve years old. Her husband was serving with the RVN[1] Army and his infrequent visits home usually resulted in another offspring. She had made mention that she was expecting another child but she didn't appear nor act at all pregnant. My assumption was that I had misinterpreted her message about having another baby.

She was eager to show us her home which was immaculately clean. One of the three rooms had five mats on the ground neatly spaced with a small pillow on each. She cooked over a charcoal stove and their bathroom was little more than an outdoor privy.

It was a revelation to me – here was a person I knew primarily as a lowly mamasan but she was so much more. Bá Klaum was a wife and a mother who worked hard to give her children a decent life. The human side of that person surfaced, and I mentally scolded myself for such shallow and stereotypical thinking. My frame of mind toward her changed radically knowing she was filling those roles.

✳✳✳✳✳

I had envied Gary Howell's stateside orders from Tech school to Seymour-Johnson AFB in North Carolina, but no sooner had he and his wife arrived and got settled in, his squadron was mobilized to Vietnam. His job was loading bombs on F-4 *Phantom* fighter jets at Cam Ranh airbase.

I received a letter from Gary asking if he could visit me. He wanted to see if everything he had heard about Nha Trang was really true – beautiful beach, shops and restaurants, great weather,

---

[1] Republic of Vietnam – South Vietnam

and live shows with round-eyed females. I wrote him back inviting him to be my guest and find out first hand.

Gary arrived on the early flight from Cam Ranh and I met him at the passenger terminal. He had seen the beach from the aircraft, as I had on my first flight in, and couldn't believe that it was really a war zone. He was astounded with the difference between his place and mine – he proclaimed a Shangri-La was only sixty miles up the coast from Cam Ranh.

He arrived on my off-duty day so my time was open to anything he wanted to see and do. The first thing Gary wanted was to visit the beach. *"Sure thing,"* I said *"but take some shoes... the sand is hot!"* We spent the morning hours at the beach and returned to the base in the early afternoon. We had missed the lunch meal so I asked Gary if he wanted to get a bite to eat at the *Playboy Club*. He was taken back at my question and said, *"The what? Do you mean like Playboy Bunnies and all that?"* I told him he was half-right and to forget about any scantly clad bunnies.

We walked over to the Army camp and entered the darkened and air conditioned club. The floorshow wouldn't begin until later that night so the only entertainment at the moment was a jukebox. We shared a pizza and a pitcher of beer, and cooled off after being in the sun all morning.

We talked a lot about different things, mostly about work. Then he said he felt as if he needed to offer me an apology. I was startled and my mind raced about why I needed an apology. I replied, *"Gary, I have no idea what you mean... there's nothing to apologize about."* He explained, *"Back at Lowery, you asked my advice about getting married before coming over here and I encouraged you to do it. I'm not sure now that was good advice because you and Barbara had to spend your first year apart."*

Gary and his wife Betty had married before he entered the Air Force and they both thought marriage was a good thing – something they highly recommended. I told Gary there were no hard feelings whatsoever and that an apology wasn't necessary. Furthermore, I told him that separation had only deepened the commitment between Barbara and me and I'm glad I married before coming to Vietnam. Gary said, *"That's good to hear... I didn't know if you were gonna shake my hand or bust my lip when we met this morning."*

That evening we took a bus downtown, which was a real revelation to Gary. I told him I would treat him to a steak dinner at a downtown eatery. We entered the *Beacon Restaurant* and the Vietnamese proprietor greeted us at the door. He thrived on American patrons to keep his business solvent because servicemen had more money to spend than the locals. He seated us under an overhead paddle fan and the breeze was welcomed. We both ordered a steak of some description – the menu was in Vietnamese. We might have ordered water buffalo, which was okay... I just didn't want dog!

Servicemen were constantly warned not to drink the water and not to eat anything raw or food that couldn't be peeled. A green salad was taboo because it was washed in unpurified water. We both ordered a "33 Beer," a locally brewed lager. The beers arrived ice cold but the smell of the brew was stifling and neither Gary nor I could finish the bottle[1]. That was my first and last 33 Beer.

Our food arrived – it was surprisingly succulent and we shared a bottle of wine with our steak. Our waiter stood quietly beside our

---

[1]   The pungent smell was reportedly from formaldehyde used in the brewing process.

table throughout our entire meal to cater to our every need. It was a little unnerving but was considered the highest level of service – much like a concierge. Our bill was very reasonable, the owner wouldn't allow a tip, and we paid him with MPC which he gladly accepted.

Afterwards we walked around a while and then caught the bus back to the airbase. Gary lodged in the transit barracks and departed the following morning. Before leaving, he thanked me for the hospitality and for not being upset with him about the marriage issue. He reminded me once again of the contrast between our work places by saying, *"Nha Trang isn't a war zone airbase…it's a resort!"* He'd change his mind if he ever experienced a mortar attack – Cam Ranh was seldom besieged with hostilities[1].

✳✳✳✳✳

I entered the barracks one afternoon to hear a GI talking down to Bá Klaum with all sorts of slurs and insults. I picked up my pace and reached him full stride and got immediately into his face. In my harshest voice I said, *"Why don't you just give it a rest? This woman works her butt off for pennies a day and she's got five kids to feed at home. I know this place is a hellhole and one day we both can leave it… but this is her home and she'll never leave it. So back off and give this woman some respect."*

The GI refuted, *"Hey man, she's just a mamasan… what do you care?"* That remark infuriated me. I got even closer to him and spoke through clenched teeth, *"This woman has more integrity in her little finger than you have in your whole body and she'd kick your ass if she could…but she can't… so I'll do it for her if I ever hear you say anything to*

---

[1] Cam Ranh Airbase was considered so safe that President Johnson visited it twice. Nevertheless, the area was jolted from its immunity when the VC raided Cam Ranh Bay in 1969, killing 2 Americans and wounding 98.

her again!" He looked at me and said almost pathetically, *"Ya know something? You've been in Vietnam way too long!"* He then turned away and left the barracks.

I looked at Bá Klaum and she acknowledged what just happened by softly saying, *"GI numba one"* as a small tear streamed down her cheek. I had a hunch that she knew all along when a GI was disgracing her. She looked away, brushed back the tear with the palm of her hand, and went back to her ironing.

The irreverent GI's comment about me being in Vietnam *"...way too long"* evoked a lot of thought on my part. Could it be that I had become overly assertive about conveying my feelings in the eight months I'd been in Vietnam or had I evolved into a person with a mentality to solve issues with physical aggression? Maybe it was some of both. What I did know was that it felt right at the time and I didn't regret saying what I did. The GI avoided Bá Klaum and me like the plague from then on.

★★★★★

An unannounced MPC change-out was again conducted in February. These events never happened at regular intervals but rather when officials believed it was needed. Once again we were issued brand new MPC that was obviously different from the old version.

Shortly after the exchange, a rumor amid the servicemen on base was that an extremely bold and clever GI went into town immediately following the MPC exchange and purchased merchandise using the play money from a Monopoly game! The local merchants hadn't seen the new MPC and they accepted the play money thinking it was bona fide MPC. The rumor further claimed the GI wisely never returned to town and that his DEROS was imminent. Leave it to a GI to finagle every possible angle to gain the upper hand!

★★★★★

When a GI's DEROS approached and he had his stateside orders, he became *"FIGMO[1]."* Most GIs counted down the remaining days using a *"FIGMO Calendar,"* which was a sketch of a very voluptuous nude female whose body was sectioned into ninety separately numbered segments – the last three in prominent locations. As the final ninety days ticked off, each day's segment on the calendar would be colored in. When she was completely painted, it was time to go home!

The long awaited day finally arrived – February 21, 1969…I was now entitled to start a FIGMO calendar! I attached a FIGMO calendar[2] to the inside door of my locker and each morning I would color the corresponding segment with a pink crayon. Slowly, my black and white sketch became vibrant.

---

[1] Finally, I Got My Orders
[2] I saved my FIGMO calendar and foolishly brought it home. Barbara thought it was repulsive.

Chapter 11

"Not Again!"

March – May 1969

"What lies behind us and what lies before us are tiny matters compared to what lies within us."
Ralph Waldo Emerson

In the News...

* *Dwight D. Eisenhower, the 34th U. S. President and retired 5-star general who led the Normandy D-Day invasion during Word War II, died at Walter Reed Army Medical Center, Washington, DC at the age of 78. He survived a half-dozen heart attacks over 15 years before succumbing to a final attack in March.*

* *The G-rated motion picture "Oliver" beat out the highly favored "Funny Girl" as Best Picture at the 41st Academy Awards held in Los Angeles on April 14. Cliff Robertson won Best Actor in "Charley" while a tie was announced for the Best Actress between Katharine Hepburn in "The Lion in Winter" and Barbra Streisand in "Funny Girl."*

* *James Earl Ray pleaded guilty to the murder of Dr. Martin Luther King and was sentenced to 99 years in jail. Ray later repudiated that plea.*

* *President Nixon proclaimed he would end the Vietnam War in 1970.*

* *The Concorde supersonic passenger airplane made its maiden flight at Filton Aerodrome, north of Bristol, England.*

* *President Nixon ordered secret bombing campaigns in Cambodia in March (code-named Operation Menu) to destroy what was believed to be the headquarters of the National Front for the Liberation of Vietnam and later escalated the conflict with secretly bombing Laos before Congress cut the funding for the conflict in Vietnam.*

* *Sirhan Sirhan was sentenced to death for assassinating New York Sen. Robert F. Kennedy. The sentence was later reduced to life imprisonment.*

* *"Marcus Welby MD," a TV series, debuted on ABC-TV. It began a popular series with Robert Young as the leading actor.*

* *Levi Straus started to market bell-bottomed jeans.*

* *U.S. military personnel in Vietnam peaked at 543,000 in April. Over 33,000 had already been killed.*

In early March my roommate for nearly ten months departed Vietnam to be honorably discharged. Despite the unsolicited advice I received long ago about not making close friends while in Vietnam, Richard and I were the best of buddies and I valued our friendship. His long-term goal was to own and operate a restaurant in Manhattan – his ambition to be a photographer dissolved with the theft of his prized camera.

He was a few years ahead of me in age but lacked the intimate family ties like those I had with my family – a relationship that he admittedly envied. Richard never exhibited any reliance or reverence to religion. I wouldn't call him an atheist – more of the agnostic type. Being a Christian, I made a point to routinely show my faith to him in a nonthreatening manner while respecting his beliefs...and his disbeliefs. Our opposing viewpoints never affected our friendship in any manner and we got along just fine.

I wished him the best of luck, shook his hand, and we both vowed to keep in touch[1]. Six days later, I received a post card from him that he had written at the Pittsburg airport while waiting for a flight. He boasted, *"I am sitting in the airport and I am a free and happy*

---

[1] We exchanged letters only once.

civilian. From now on, you will call me <u>Mister</u> Bush!" I was going to miss my buddy.

When Richard vacated the barracks, I immediately claimed the lower (and safer) bunk for myself – for the first time in my Air Force career I would occupy a bed closer to the floor than to the ceiling. The upper berth didn't stay empty very long – an Airman named John Penzone arrived the next day and I welcomed him… not because I was that hospitable but because he, now being the most junior man in the barracks, would inherent my water jug duty.

Maybe it was our brief time together or maybe our dissimilar personalities, but John and I never really connected as friends the way Richard and I had during our tour together. In all likelihood, he couldn't wait for my departure so he could claim the lower berth. In eighty-two days, he could gladly have it!

★★★★★

Another short-lived vacancy occurred in the barracks that gave another Airman the opportunity to move into the *Flightline Hilton.* The boyish GI, who was big for his age and lumbering to the point of clumsiness, couldn't have been more than eighteen years old. His name was Alexander but because he was pudgy, he was tagged with the facetious nickname of *"The Marshmallow."* He was naïve and gullible to anything, and sadly some GIs took full advantage of his innocence. The best thing that could happen to Alex would be puberty.

He was exceedingly edgy about being in a war zone. Realizing his paranoia about mortar attacks, a few guys compounded his uneasiness by telling war stories that were overly exaggerated. He often wore his flak vest to bed and sometimes his helmet too. He became the brunt of some mean-spirited practical jokes – a GI would sneak up behind him and pop a paper bag just to see him fall to the floor and whimper.

An inevitable mortar attack happened only three weeks after his arrival. The brief assault was short lived and was over in less than a half hour. When the all-clear signal was sounded, we returned to our bunks to salvage some shut-eye before dawn. I hoped the relentless ribbing would cease now that Alex was a veteran of a bona fide attack.

Everything had become still and quiet when we heard a muffled moan from the vicinity of Alex's cubicle. His roommate called out for help and several of us hurried to the area to find Alex *under* his bunk bed and he couldn't get out. During the first few minutes of the attack, he mustered enough adrenalin to lift the heavy bunk bed completely off the floor and crawl underneath! Following the attack, he was unable to raise the bed with his normal strength, so four of us had to lift the bed to allow him to make an exit.

That astounding feat of strength proved to be very advantageous for Alex because he displayed almost superhuman strength which squelched most all putdowns in fear he'd use his muscle against any GI who taunted him. His new nickname eventually became *"Baby Huey[1]."*

★★★★★

A master sergeant arrived at the squadron and was assigned to a new position called "Dock Chief," but he immediately assumed the self-appointed role as a quality control expert. His presence became a point of contention with most all the work centers that, for the most part, were self-supervised and already had a senior

---

[1] Baby Huey was a gigantic and naïve infant cartoon character who possessed exceptional strength.

NCO in charge. The egotistical newcomer really thought he was a gift to the squadron and without his influence, we were all a blundering bunch of peons in dire need of his guidance and supervision.

He would repeatedly go behind us to scrutinize our work and identify menial insignificant issues that had no bearing on mission priority. He was once quoted as saying, *"No aircraft will leave my docks with any write-ups!"* His docks? Since when were they his docks? We were justifiably proud of the low percentage of discrepancies we had achieved before his arrival and at no time did we need his guidance or supervision!

Everyone in the Armament work center lamented to Sgt. Baker about this self-centered jerk. Sgt. Baker said he'd investigate the matter and then have a meeting to discuss it. The next day, he called us all together, even the guys on the late shift, and told us there was little he could do about the situation. We couldn't believe it – that guy was hampering our quality of work, not helping it. Sgt. Baker explained, *"Everything he's writing up is justified. I'm not saying it's necessarily the right thing to do... basically he's correct according to the Technical Orders. The man has done his homework."* There just had to be a way to combat that tyrant.

We all knew what was important and crucial in our armament discipline, and we made great strides to ensure these areas had our foremost concern. Small trivial matters were often disregarded – we were complying with the intent rather than the letter of the Tech Order.

Soon afterwards, we had another meeting without Sgt. Baker. We all agreed that the Dock Chief would relentlessly examine our work until he found at least one discrepancy, regardless of how menial the finding. He was obsessed to find *something* wrong in each area of the aircraft. Supposedly that would make him appear favorable to the Maintenance Officer and perhaps justify his job or perhaps be grounds for a promotion.

We then realized a pattern had developed – once he found the first item not to his liking… he'd quit looking and move on to a different area of the aircraft for more scrutiny. One of my cohorts came up with a brilliant strategy – if he's so intent to find something wrong… *let's give it to him!* The plan was to deliberately bait him with at least one "token" issue so he could check his box and move on. We'd make a game of it… and that way we'd be in control of the situation instead of the situation being in control of us. (Where had I heard that before?)

Beginning the next day, we intentionally installed undersized cotter pins, safety wire without enough twists-per-inch, incorrect torque settings, oversized hardware, etc… anything to create a write-up. We were cognizant to correct all the "bait issues" if he failed to identify them. When the real Quality Control inspector performed the final check of the aircraft, no such issues were identified, making the Dock Chief look foolish and incompetent.

Our plan worked like a dream and the scheme spread quickly through the other work centers. They began using their own "bait tactic" which worked equally well and achieved the same results. We even divulged our ploy to Sgt. Baker and he loved it… but was quick to say he would deny any knowledge of such a tactic if ever questioned.

Eventually, the Maintenance Officer came to realize the selfish ulterior motives of that individual and that his antics were counter-productive to the squadron. The Dock Chief was quietly reassigned to a desk job – much to the delight of all the dockworkers.

*****

When I answered the Maintenance Control hot-line telephone in the armament shop, I recognized the voice instantly – it was Capt. Richardson, one of the FCF pilots with whom I had flown backseat on several occasions. He remembered a comment I made about wanting to take a flight in an O-2A before my departure in May. He said an FCF was scheduled for a *Skymaster* that afternoon and invited me to fly with him. That was an unexpected opportunity that I couldn't pass up.

Sgt. Baker approved the flight, and I met Capt. Richardson at the aircraft. Unlike the Bird Dog's inline seating, the O-2A's pilot and observer seats were tandem (side-by-side), with the pilot in the left seat. When he started both engines and taxied to the runway, I noticed immediately that the O-2A was much quieter due to the closed fuselage.

We received our take off clearance and Capt. Richardson revved both engines and released the wheel brakes. The aircraft literally jumped from its starting position and quickly accelerated down the runway. It was a smooth and quiet ride as we gracefully lifted off the asphalt departing southeast towards the ocean. All was going great – for the moment.

Shortly after take-off, Capt. Richardson raised the gear lever in the cockpit to retract the tricycle landing gear. Immediately a flurry of hydraulics was heard as the nose gear tucked neatly into the fuselage with one fluid motion and locked with a noticeable thud. But something went amiss with the two main gears. The gears normally cycle through three distinctive motions before they disappear into the fuselage, but our landing gear seized after going through only one stage. I imagined the airplane looked like a seagull in flight with two broken legs dandling beneath.

Capt. Richardson peered out his side window and saw the crippled left-main gear hanging limp. He told me to look at the gear on my side, and to my utter dismay, I saw the same thing. He then pushed down the gear lever in an attempt to extend the gear. The two main gears and the nose gear responded and extended to their normal gear-down position.

But there was still a problem – we didn't have a gear-lock indication on the instrument panel which meant the main gears were not secure. Without a locked gear, the aircraft could possibly collapse to the runway when any weight was placed on the landing gear. There was no doubt we had a crippled bird that posed a serious circumstance. I thought to myself, *"Why did I ever want to ride in a Skymaster?"*

I asked Capt. Richardson about our options. He cited three possible scenarios – none of which appealed to me: ditch the aircraft in the ocean, crash land on the runway, or take our chances that the gear would support the aircraft's weight when we landed. Bailing out was not an option since neither of us had parachutes.

He radioed the control tower and declared an emergency that prompted the crash crews to scramble to both sides of the runway. We made several low, slow passes over the control tower and the controllers examined the *Skymaster* with binoculars. They reported our gear appeared fully extended, but they couldn't determine whether or not it was locked.

The next thirty minutes were spent burning fuel to lessen the chance of a fire if we did indeed crash land. We circled over the ocean in what seemed like an eternity. The fuel burn wait was excruciating – I wanted to get it over with!

It goes without saying that it was a time of high anxiety for me. My heart was pounding and I had to deliberately take some slow deep breaths to ease my nervousness. I silently appealed to my ever-present Guardian Angel to grant us a safe return to the ground. My personal Protector had yet to betray me and that definitely was a time of need for me.

I peered out the window at the shoreline far below and perceived the beach to be a haven of safety. I would have gladly exchanged places with anybody on firm ground at that moment. Finally Capt. Richardson made an approach to the runway. He told me he was going to bounce the aircraft's weight on the gear to see if it would buckle and that no attempt would be made to land the aircraft. He warned me if the gear did collapse, we might be forced to make a belly landing. He flew the O-2A over the runway and tested the gear by lowering the aircraft down several times. The gear seemed to be okay but we still weren't receiving the lock indication that would assure us the gear was safe. We returned to the sky for another try.

Capt. Richardson said, *"Okay, this time we're gonna stop... one way or another!"* We circled and approached the runway again. He gently put weight on the gear but this time he cut back the throttles. I held my breath and cringed for a crash. To my sheer relief, the aircraft was rolling down the runway supporting itself with its landing gear! We braked to a full stop and I gazed up at the sky and whispered a brief prayer of gratefulness. Once again, He came through for me.

The control tower cancelled the emergency and the crash crew returned to their quarters. We taxied back to the squadron area and several mechanics met us at the revetment. When I exited the plane, I was drenched with perspiration. Then I saw that Capt. Richardson was also sopping wet so I didn't feel too embarrassed about the sweat.

As it turned out, an improperly rigged tie rod caused the mishap. The landing gear had always been locked but never gave us the indication in the cockpit. Someone's butt was going to be barbecued due to the incident and I certainly was glad it wasn't mine!

✭✭✭✭✭

The U.S. Armed Forces widely promoted a unique program enticing the Viet Cong to defect to the side of allied forces. This amnesty plan, known as Chieu Hoi[1] (pronounced *"Choo Hoy"*), was publicized through several mediums – leaflets were scattered over suspected enemy locations by helicopters or special "pysops" aircraft that were also equipped with aerial loudspeakers; the waterproof ammunition pouches discarded on the battlefield by U.S. GIs contained printed information on them about Chieu Hoi; and information about the plan was broadcast over Armed Forces Television and Radio Network.

Young Vietnamese males were forced into service by the Viet Cong (much like the U.S. Selective Service Draft). The typical recruit was fifteen to twenty-five years of age, had little or no education, and was a farmer or hired laborer before becoming a Viet Cong guerrilla. Because many of the recruits were pressed into service, the VC morale was usually low – again, much like draftees in the U.S. Armed Forces.

These "drafted" Viet Cong guerrillas were the primary focal group of the Chieu Hoi program which guaranteed safe passage and provided care and protection for the defectors. Former VC guerrillas would often be integrated into allied units as scouts

---

[1] Chieu Hoi is literally translated as *"Open Arms."*

operating in the same area where they had once been as a Viet Cong.

★★★★★

A brand new Second Lieutenant fresh from ROTC arrived at the squadron and was assigned to perform menial tasks which didn't require much expertise. Among those chores was inspecting each junior enlisted man's personal space for any contraband – a real pain in the butt for most GIs. Such inspections seldom disclosed any dangerous or unauthorized items.

On the announced date of the inspection (which was unbelievably dumb), the eager neophyte officer arrived at 0530 hours to begin his search. When he reached my cubicle, I opened my locker and stood back as he looked through all my belongings. The locker had a shelf about four inches from the top that could have easily hidden something if placed in the back. *"Is there anything on that top shelf?"* he asked. *"No sir, that shelf is empty,"* I replied. He looked at me as if he just knew he'd found something. *"Then you shouldn't mind at all if I take a look myself,"* he said in his most authoritative tone of voice. I said, *"Sir, you can look if you want to…but I wouldn't recommend it."*

"Bring me a chair!" he ordered. I brought a chair from the Day Room and placed it directly in front of the locker. *"Sir, I really wouldn't recommend doing this,"* I advised. He ignored my warning and climbed in the chair in a crouched position and slowly stood up. I knew what was about to happen and sure enough… *WHAP*, the ceiling paddle fan struck him across his forehead! The blow almost knocked him off the chair. He grabbed his forehead as I helped him off the chair. Once on the floor, he sat down in the chair and appeared to be in a daze. I was surprised the whack didn't break his skin.

I just had to say, *"Sir, that's why I keep nothing on that top shelf."* Without saying a word, the officer stood up and staggered out of the barracks still clutching his swollen forehead. After he left, the GIs in the barracks burst out with uncontrollable laughter.

I had to chuckle thinking about the morning's staff meeting and how he'd explain the red streak across his forehead. Surely he wouldn't admit to the Squadron Commander that he was stupid enough to stick his head into a spinning paddle fan!

*****

Neither Barbara nor I had ever owned an automobile, so I asked her to shop around and purchase one before I came home. We needed a car for the cross-country trip from Atlanta to Las Vegas, and I didn't want us to make a hasty decision upon my return. Barbara's Dad was a top-notch auto mechanic so I knew he'd thoroughly check out any car Barbara picked out. She was more interested in appearance and accessories rather than in mechanical integrity, and I think her Dad nixed a few of her early choices.

After shopping around, she finally found a vehicle that satisfied both her and her Dad – a 1967 Dodge Cornett 440. Her letter described it as: V-8, two-door, white with a black vinyl top, power steering, and air-conditioned (almost a necessity in the hot Nevada desert). She made a down payment and financed the balance for three years through her credit union with payments of $47 per month. The total price of the two-year old car was $2,150.

*****

The staff sergeant was late for duty again. He had a tendency for being tardy – mostly due to a hangover. His habitual drinking created such chronic problems that he was forced to live on base instead of a downtown villa where most NCOs had the privilege to reside. His NCOIC tolerated his delinquency because, once sober, he was a valuable and effective member of the work center. I had worked with him a few times but he was an acquaintance rather than a friend.

On that particular morning, the NCOIC waited thirty minutes and then sent two of his co-workers to his barracks to get him out of bed. They returned shortly thereafter and reported, *"We can't wake him...he must be unconscious."*

The man wasn't unconscious – he was dead. He had succumbed in his sleep after downing a fifth of bourbon the previous night. In Vietnam, booze was plentiful and inexpensive, and the sergeant had an acute addiction. Those two factors resulted in a tragic outcome.

The news spread like wildfire throughout the work centers. The topic of conversation centered around his drinking – no one could remember when they ever saw him eat anything... he drank most of his meals. Comments about that incident varied from *"That poor soul"* to *"Serves him right!"*

What a tragic waste of a human life. Sure, that man was an adult and responsible for his own actions... but somebody should have intervened and been proactive at some point to prevent that tragedy. To die in Vietnam due to alcoholism was such a disgrace and so preventable. The incident should have brought light to the seriousness of addiction. It didn't. There were hordes of GIs strung out on booze and dope and nobody seemed to care.

✶✶✶✶✶

Easter had always been a sacred time for me and I wanted to continue my reverence to this hallowed occasion. I was delighted to hear about an Easter sunrise service on the beach – a perfect location to view the sunrise. Shuttle buses from the airbase to the beach began at 0515 hours – the official time for sunrise on Easter (April 6) was 0609 hours. It was a brisk and breezy morning with sparse clouds. I was surprised to see so many Vietnamese in attendance until I realized the Vietnamese Catholic Church was conducting the service. I looked around for Bá Klaum but if she was there, I didn't see her.

The choir was an all-female group of about a dozen, all wearing very attractive Áo dài tunics that were being jostled by the gusty sea breeze. Fortunately, the service was bilingual with every part spoken first in Vietnamese and then in English. After a good size crowd of about fifty people gathered, the service began with Scripture reading and songs – all sang in English. It was a very special moment for me when the sun broke the watery horizon. I savored the moment knowing that experiencing an Easter Sunday sunrise over the South China Sea was probably a once-in-a-lifetime event for me.

★★★★★

On April 9, something happened that I had been longing for nearly a year – my replacement arrived! He was a three striper "buck sergeant" from somewhere in Michigan. Sgt. Baker assigned me as his trainer and I was more than ready to bring him up to speed. The newcomer wanted to live off base with many of the other NCOs but he was one stripe shy of that privilege.

It was disturbing to me that the guy lacked any eagerness or enthusiasm for his new assignment. He was flippant and carefree about most every aspect of his work. One time when he became overly annoyed about having to clean a rocket launcher, I told him that it was a part of the job and to get use to it. His reply was, _"Hey…what will they do to me….send me to Vietnam?"_

Maybe he expected a more defining contribution to the war effort as evidenced by his indifferent attitude toward the 21st TASS. His attitude was an insult to me...I didn't realize until then my degree of loyalty to the crucial mission of the FACs.

★★★★★

April's Commander's Call was held in the Chapel and attendance was mandatory – the largest crowd I'd ever seen in the sanctuary. As previously announced, I was presented a small trophy for the Munitions Man of the Quarter award. The trophy itself depicted a man in a fatigue uniform supposedly holding a toolbox in his right hand, but it looked more like

a lunchbox to me. After a brief round of applause, I thanked the Colonel for the award and returned to my seat.

No sooner than I had sat down, Col. Forster again called me to the front. He said, *"This comes as a total surprise for Airman Moss, and it gives me pleasure to announce that he was also selected for the Semi-Annual Munitions Man Award and is deserving of another trophy!"* He then presented me with an identical trophy as before except a little larger – same guy, same lunchbox. The Colonel added, *"This recognition is accompanied by a personal letter from General George S. Brown, the Commander of the Pacific 7th Air Force granting Airman Moss a three-day pass to any in-country location."*

Just when the teasing had subsided from the last award, now this! I really couldn't believe I had beat out every other munitions man in the 7th Air Force for that honor. I saw firsthand those load crews in Cam Ranh busting their butts twelve hours a day with no time off. How possibly could I have exceeded their contribution? The only explanation I could imagine was that everyone was too busy to submit a nomination. As undeserving as I felt, I humbly accepted the second trophy and the three-day pass.

I know it may appear ungrateful on my part... but a three-day pass anywhere in a war zone really wasn't all that exciting to me. I wondered why it couldn't have included an R&R destination. I thought about visiting Saigon, the capitol of South Vietnam, but the hassle wouldn't be worth the effort. Then I realized I was already at a prime resort area at Nha Trang so I decided to spend three off-duty days in my own backyard. I submitted my request to Sgt. Baker for the dates (April 9 to 11), which were Wednesday through Friday. Sgt. Baker approved the request and the time off would begin the following week.

Those off-duty days were really revitalizing – I didn't realize how much I needed a break. During my time off, I played the organ at the Chapel, caught up on my reading and sleep, and relaxed unhurriedly at the beach while listening to soothing music on my radio. On Thursday, the ocean was off-limits due to a shark sighting but the beach was available for lounging.

After one particular beach visit, I was standing next to the roadway waiting for the bus to return to the base. An Air Force staff car slowed to a stop and the lone occupant asked, *"Going to the airbase?"* I didn't know the driver but I most certainly noticed his rank – Full Bird Colonel! *"Yes sir,"* I replied. The officer said, *"Hop in... I'll give you a lift."* I couldn't believe a Colonel was offering me a ride in his staff car! *"Sir, maybe that's not a good idea... my swimsuit is wet."* He replied, *"Nonsense! It won't be the first time the seat got wet."*

I opened the passenger door and sat down beside the Colonel in the front seat. During the short ride, he struck up a cordial conversation and asked me about my hometown, how long before my DEROS, how things were going for me, and other trivial questions. I commented that it had been months since I'd ridden in a car. It was a pleasant ten minutes and I thanked him repeatedly for the lift.

He insisted on taking me directly to the squadron area even though I could have easily walked there from anywhere on base. When he dropped me off in the squadron, I thanked him one last time and nervously shook his hand (I should have saluted). He said, *"Take care now and keep yourself safe."* He waved out the window as he drove away.

I stood motionless until the staff car was out of sight and then turned to see about a dozen GIs standing like statues in total awe over what they had witnessed. Without a word, I made my way through the group acting like it was an everyday occurrence for me to ride in a staff car with a Bird Colonel.

It wasn't five minutes later that I got summoned to the Orderly Room. I reported to the First Sergeant still wearing my damp swimsuit. He called me into his office, shut the door, and asked harshly, *"Would you care to tell me what the hell that was all about?"* I played dumb and said, *"What was what all about?"* He angrily replied, *"You know damn well what I'm referring to…you being chauffeured around the airbase by the Wing Commander!"* The Wing Commander? Wow! So that's who he was.

I had a perfect opportunity to fabricate some cockeyed story about what good friends we were as a result of my recognition for the PACAF's Munitions Man Award. I wisely decided against it, so I told the First Sergeant exactly what happened – the Colonel was just extending a good deed to a lowly enlisted man. I'm not sure he believed my story… but if an element of suspicion was aroused, I wanted to take full advantage of the situation. Maybe the First Sergeant would now have a whole different rapport with me.

He dismissed me but before I reached the door he said, *"Please tell me you saluted the Wing Commander."* I replied, *"Nope, we shook hands and he waved bye to me as he drove away."* He cringed and said, *"Get the hell outta here!"*

★★★★★

In the early morning hours of April 21, twenty-nine days before my departure, I was instantly awakened by the first detonation. *"Not again!"* I verbalized my dismay. *"I really don't need this crap… not now!"* I rolled to the floor as loudspeakers wailed out the alarm. My roommate joined me on the concrete as more enemy mortars fell from the predawn sky. A barrage of mortar detonations rattled the Army installation and then the enemy's target shifted to our flightline.

I had been through that scenario at least a dozen times… but things were different this time. Mortar attacks were never routine and this one was no exception. However, this particular attack *frightened* me beyond belief! My DEROS was less than a month away and the idea of me becoming injured (or killed) at such a late date was totally unacceptable.

We continued to take cover on the floor as more mortars exploded. I cringed and stiffened at each detonation while muttering a mixture of prayers and profanity throughout the attack. I kept thinking about my last words to Barbara in Hawaii, *"I'll see you in May!"* I desperately wanted to uphold that obligation.

John became aware of my uncharacteristic anxiety and asked, *"Hey man, are you okay? You're acting really strange."* I told him I'd be all right when those damn mortars stopped exploding around us. I wanted to go home alive!

The attack seemed to last an eternity – but actually it was only forty minutes. One mortar fell short of the flightline and hit the roadway near the Chapel. A row of parked jeeps became victims of shrapnel and all of them suffered flat tires and broken windshields. I was visibly shaken by the assault and became paranoid to the extent that I wore my flak vest for the remainder of the night. May 21st couldn't arrive quickly enough!

Later that day, I retrieved the ragged ribbon which had been in my locker for the past eight months and proudly tied it through the top button hole of my fatigues. It looked good and it felt good! It was official... I was a "Short-Timer!"

★★★★★

In late April, some new arrivals checked into the squadron, one of whom I immediately recognized. He was my former squad leader from basic training back at Lackland AFB. That guy was an arrogant and power-hungry snot that loved to bark out orders and impose harsh disciplinary action on his squad members – and everyone despised him. He dealt me misery for eight long weeks at Lackland ... but now I had the upper hand. I'm usually not a revengeful person, but I simply couldn't pass up an opportunity for some little payback.

As he and his companions were leaving the squadron area in route to the transit barracks, I began to follow behind them. I finally said, *"Hey Taylor, you remember me from basic?"* He stopped and turned around while the others continued on their way. He looked at me and replied, *"Uh...no I don't...should I?"* I stepped a little closer, hoping he'd notice my short-timers ribbon and looked him straight in the eyes. *"I was one of your flunky squad members back at Lackland. My name is Moss... and you made me scrub a stairwell in the barracks with my toothbrush... twice. I remember it well."*

To my delight he became squeamish, so I added, *"You being a FNG and all, I think it's only right to offer you a piece of advice."* He replied in a humble voice, *"I'll take any advice you care to give me."* I relied, *"Wherever you go, whatever you do, regardless of the time of day or night, and even in your sleep, you need to keep this in mind ... Beware! You'll never know when someone is about to attack you!"*

His eyes got wide and every ounce of blood drained from his face. I could sense the fright building up within him and I'm sure he wondered if the Viet Cong would be stalking him ...or would it be me! That generic bit of advice should add greatly to his newcomer anxiety.

Without a word he turned and caught up with his buddies. I returned to my barracks with a sense of closure on the issue. I had no intentions of pursuing the matter any further. I felt like any other squad member from basic training, if given the chance, would also take retribution against that jerk – only they'd take physical rather than psychological revenge. I chose the latter because of the lasting effects.

✸✸✸✸✸

As time drew near toward my departure, I showed Bá Klaum a calendar, pointed to Wednesday, May 21 and said, *"GI Đi đi mău"* which meant I would be quickly leaving on that date. She turned away without saying a word and appeared to sulk over my remark. That was one of the few times she ever showed any kind of moodiness. I suppose the fact she displayed regret over my departure should have told me how much she valued our friendship. I felt certain she knew I'd leave Vietnam one day … but I didn't believe she'd act that way about it.

We had a special relationship that I appreciated and I suppose it was understandable for her to deny the inevitable. That really bothered me because she made me feel as if I was somehow betraying her. For the remainder of my time, she would barely speak to me or even acknowledge my presence… and that hurt.

*****

One day I noticed a brown band of defoliated vegetation that resembled a giant ribbon that had been stretched across the mountain slopes near Nha Trang. I later discovered the swath of dead vegetation was caused by a potent herbicide called *"Agent Orange*[1]*."* The defoliant was sprayed from converted C-123 cargo aircraft[2] in a military operation called *Ranch Hand.*

The primary purpose for the defoliant was to deny cover for enemy forces and to destroy crops needed for sustenance. The areas sprayed often were those along highways and railroads to make it more difficult for the VC to ambush convoys.

These Ranch Hand aircraft were shot at from the ground as much and often as any Bird Dog, but because of their larger size, they were constantly taking more hits. Another reason was because the Ranch Hand aircraft had to fly low and slow – 150 feet above the treetops at 130 knots (only 10 knots above stall speed). The slogan for operation *Ranch Hand* was a whimsical *"Only We Can Prevent Forests."*

---

[1] The total amount of Agent Orange used near Nha Trang was said to be nearly 8,000 gallons. Between 1962 and 1971, the American military sprayed more than 19 million gallons of chemical defoliants in South Vietnam.

[2] One C-123 could spray 11,000 lbs of defoliant agent over 300 acres in four minutes.

★★★★★

I had made a reservation at the MARS station for my monthly call to Barbara. When I arrived, the lone operator said the station was down due to technical difficulties. I asked him specifically what the problem was, but being an operator and not a radioman, he said he didn't know. All he knew was the transmitter had conked out.

Being a licensed HAM Radio operator, I offered to check out the transmitter at the chance I could repair it. The operator gladly accepted my offer and told me to enter the radio room via a rear entrance. When I entered the room, I couldn't believe it – the room was *air-conditioned!* I had been living and working only a half block from air conditioning... and didn't know it. I asked the operator how the MARS station ranked such a privilege. He said the cool air wasn't for "creature comfort" but rather to prevent the electronic equipment from overheating. For whatever reason, it felt wonderful!

I began troubleshooting the ailing transmitter – a Collins KWM-2 transceiver. After a while, I diagnosed the problem as a faulty power amplifier vacuum tube. I checked the spare parts inventory, located a new 6146 vacuum tube, and replaced the suspected one. I was delighted that the transmitter restored as good as new. The operator thanked me many times and invited me to stick around just in case something else broke. I gladly obliged.

I made my call to Barbara – the operator moved my reservation to the top of the list. The radio reception was near perfect without much static. We talked beyond my allotted time limit and spoke mostly of my imminent departure which was less than sixty days!

The operator told me they were shorthanded and the MARS station was soliciting volunteers to run nightly phone patches to the  States. Without hesitation, I offered my help. After learning the proper protocol, I spent many late-night hours at the MARS station helping GIs talk to their loved ones. I volunteered for two reasons – it gave me the opportunity to work with electronics again, but probably the real reason was that I treasured the air conditioning.

One night while running a phone patch, I made an embarrassing blunder. The radio reception wasn't ideal because atmospheric static made the signal barely discernable. During the first few minutes of any MARS call, the topic of conversation was generally generic and predictable – *"How are you doing? How's the weather? Do you need anything? I really miss you."* On one particular call, I had patched a sergeant to his wife in Illinois and the usual questions were being asked. Everything was routine until the wife asked, *"Did you get Amy's package? Over."* The sergeant answered, *"Who's Amy? Over."* She replied, *"Amy… your daughter! Over!"*

At that moment I knew something wasn't kosher. Both the stateside MARS operator and I momentarily disconnected the patch. He asked me which listing was on the phone. When I told him, I realized I had put the wrong person on the line… the sergeant was talking to someone else's wife!

To make matters worse, the radio signal dropped out altogether so I couldn't make amends. I apologized to the sergeant and as he was leaving the waiting area, he walked past the lone Airman who was my next listing. He casually asked the Airman, *"Did you get Amy's package?"* The startled Airman looked up and replied, *"Uh… yeah. But how did you…"* The sergeant replied as he was leaving the station, *"Your wife still loves you."*

★★★★★

The Vietnamese language was next to impossible for me to learn because it's tonal – how you say something is just as important as what you say. To add to the confusion, dialects varied between the regions of the country, much like my southern accent does in the United States.

Vietnamese is also a monosyllabic language. Each syllable expresses a distinct idea and therefore is a word in itself. Often two or more syllables are joined to form new words, as in location names like Sia-gon and Ha-noi. For those reasons, it was very difficult for me to pick up the language other than the simple phrases I learned to communicate with Bá Klaum. She once tried to teach me the days of the week but two of the days sounded exactly the same so I quit trying.

Vietnamese was first written in Chinese characters, but during the 17th century, missionaries converted the written language into the Latin alphabet. Both forms were used until 1920 when the Latin script was officially adopted. The language consists of twelve vowels and twenty-seven consonants – another reason I had problems learning the vernacular[1].

---

[1] 27 million people spoke Vietnamese as a first language.

★★★★★

The rocket aiming device on an O-1 E/F aircraft lacked the sophistication of a jet fighter aircraft, or an O-2A *Skymaster*. The aiming procedure was rudimentary at best – a foot-long metal rod was attached to the top engine cowling which protruded upward into the pilot's field of view. The pilot aligned the rod with a circular ring inside the fuselage, much like the rear and front sights of any rifle.

An O-1E came into the phase docks with a write-up on the aiming device. The complaint was that fired rockets were tracking *"half-a-click left of the rocket sight."* The author of that write-up apparently believed there was some elaborate bore-sighting procedure to assure the accuracy of the rocket sight. In actuality, the problem was caused by a skewed front sighting rod. All I did to correct the problem was to hold the rod in my bare hand and bend it slightly to the right – no tools or alignment device needed. I signed off the write-up in the aircraft's logbook with the corrective action stated as *"Corrected rocket aiming device."*

When the aircraft came out of the docks, the FCF pilot reviewed the logbook and noticed the write-up and corrective action taken. He called our work center and wanted to talk with the person who corrected that deficiency. He said the write-up warranted a rocket fire test and he wanted me to ride back seat to see if indeed the problem had been corrected.

I arrived at the revetment before the pilot and loaded the Bird Dog with rockets. He arrived and performed a thorough preflight inspection – an absolute necessity following a phase inspection. We boarded the aircraft and ten minutes later we were airborne over the rural countryside northwest of the city. The pilot radioed *"Ragged Scooper"* and was granted permission for a rocket fire in the quadrant we were currently occupying. I saw no occupation of any kind in the area – no people, no animals, and no evidence of any military activity.

He brought the Bird Dog down low over a small river and told me over the intercom to help him identify a definitive target. The river was lined with lush vegetation without any target candidates. After a while, we passed a supposedly abandoned shack on the riverbank and the pilot said, *"Looks like we got a target!"*

We gained altitude and the pilot executed a textbook rocket run. He armed the armament system and then selected the two outermost rockets. During our descent, he carefully aligned the riverside shack with the Bird Dog's aiming device and pulled the trigger on the control stick. Immediately, the two selected rockets fired and went screaming toward the shack – both were direct hits! The result was an initial fireball followed by the characteristic cloud of white smoke. The pilot exclaimed, *"Bingo!"* as we pulled out of the dive.

We circled and returned to the impact area for an assessment. Neither of us were expecting to see what we saw – *chickens*...a flock of slain chickens! *We had attacked a chicken house!* Debris from the burning shack was strewn over the area and dead chickens were everywhere. The shack collapsed, tumbled into the river, and began to drift slowly downstream still ablaze with its entourage of foul companions. The pilot exclaimed, *"Oh shit, we gotta get the hell outta here!"* We made a hasty retreat and headed back to the airbase.

I was pleased that I had accurately adjusted the rocket sight but had remorse over the damage we had caused. It was obvious that we had demolished someone's chicken house – the owner probably gained access to the shack via the river since there were no roads or pathways on land. Raising chickens was probably a decent source of income and now it was gone – destroyed by the "Ugly Americans."

On a lighter note, the unmerciful but good-natured taunting from the other pilots over that incident was relentless. The FCF pilot was tagged with the call sign of *Colonel Sanders* and escalated to the point of having a dead chicken stenciled on the door of his Bird Dog.

★★★★★

Personnel assigned to Forward Operating Locations (FOL) often had to perform a variety of tasks, some of which were outside their area of expertise. One of these jobs was uploading and downloading aircraft rockets on FAC aircraft. Before they could officially perform that job, they had to be field-certified by attending a daylong class on safe handling and loading of rocket ordinance. That training was usually performed in a group setting, but now it was required to be accomplished by each individual TASS squadron.

Sgt Baker approached me about conducting the training for our squadron. I was very apprehensive about that assignment – most all of the attendees would be at least two grades above me, and I had reservations about my credibility. Sgt. Baker said credibility shouldn't be a concern and that he would monitor my first couple of classes. I instantly picked up the word "couple," which prompted my next question, *"How many classes will I teach?"* He said classes would be a weekly event until all FOL personnel were certified – maybe after a dozen sessions.

I regarded that assignment as payback for receiving the Munitions Maintenance Man award, and I was in no position to refuse. I reluctantly accepted the job and asked for a syllabus or lesson plan for the course. I was stunned when he said no such syllabus existed and that I'd have to make my own lesson plan. Then Sgt. Baker told me I needed to get busy because the first class was in three days! *"Oh yeah I almost forgot,"* he added, *"You'll also need to create some kind of written exam for your students."* What in the world had I agreed to?

I hurriedly reviewed the Technical Orders and safety regulations to formulate a lesson plan. I suggested to Sgt. Baker that I conduct the class in the squadron's pilot briefing room – the only room with chairs, podium, and a chalkboard. The first part of the day would be devoted to technical matters and safety. After lunch we would go out to the flightline and actually load rockets. We would then return to the classroom for the written exam and course critique. Sgt. Baker agreed to all my suggestions.

Three days later, I arrived early to prepare the classroom. I had several teaching aids, including an inert rocket, for my show-and-tell morning session. I could feel my anxiety rising as two-dozen servicemen filed in the room at the appointed hour. Among the attendees was the former "Dock Tyrant" who dealt me so much misery a few months ago. What a strange twist of fate – I hoped he remembered me. My heart skipped a beat when two lieutenants entered the classroom. Nobody said anything about officers in my class! I figured I'd either make a complete fool of myself or be the best E-3 instructor they'd ever seen!

I swallowed hard and made my introduction, *"Good morning gentlemen, I'm Airman First Class Dean Moss and I'll be your instructor for this training today. The subject matter is very important in that you'll be handling highly volatile ordinance. All safety regulations must be strictly adhered to... your first mistake could be your last mistake. So please be attentive and ask questions if you don't understand any portion of today's training."* I looked in the rear of the classroom and Sgt. Baker gave me a silent "thumbs-up" signal. I looked around the classroom and saw that I had the attention and respect of everyone there – even the officers. With newfound confidence, I began the training and offered the class all the information and safety matters they needed to perform their job.

During the lecture, one of the officers asked a question and I prefaced my answer with a *"Sir."* It was ingrained in me since ROTC to address all officers in that manner. The lieutenant said, *"In this setting, I'm your student and you're my instructor. You can leave off the Sir for now."* I acknowledged his comment with an embarrassing *"Yes Sir"* which got a hearty laugh from the class.

Following lunch, we performed hands-on training as each student had the opportunity to load and download live rockets. The written exam was very basic and just about everyone aced it (except one of the officers and the former Dock Tyrant). Following the exam I solicited a written critique from the class and most obliged.

When the last student exited the classroom, I breathed a sigh of relief and was glad that was behind me. Sgt. Baker entered the room and noticed my relaxed posture and asked, *"Were you aware the Squadron Commander monitored the class from the back of the room this morning?"* I was unaware of that special visitor and thankfully so – I would have been a basket case had I known.

Sgt. Baker looked over the critiques and after a few moments said, *"If you had any doubt as to your qualifications to teach this class, take a look at these critiques."* Most everyone had submitted a critique sheet and each one had some very flattering comments. One sergeant said I had made a boring subject interesting and that he learned a lot. One of the officers said I was well versed in the subject matter and was an exceptional trainer. These comments boosted my ego to the sky! In all, I taught eight classes – one a week until my

DEROS. Another person from our work center monitored my last two classes as an understudy before he taught the remainder of the classes.

★★★★★

One afternoon I found Bá Klaum doubled over on the floor in pain. I picked her up in my arms and gently placed her on my bunk. Her discomfort was so intense she couldn't communicate with me. Not knowing exactly what to do, I summoned the mamasan from the next barracks and she rushed to Bá Klaum's bedside. The two women conversed briefly while I stood by helplessly. Then I heard a word that was totally unexpected – _Babysan!_

My first thoughts were, _"No...no, this cannot be happening. Bá Klaum is having a baby at this moment... and she's in my bed!"_ Bá Klaum told me she was expecting a baby but I didn't believe her. Most pregnant women I've seen were noticeably sizeable and had difficulty moving about as the delivery date neared. Bá Klaum never showed any signs of expecting a child.

I rushed across the road to the squadron's Orderly Room and bolted through the door. _"I gotta see the First Sergeant now!"_ I told the clerk behind a desk. He replied, _"No can do Airman...he's in a staff meeting behind closed doors, not to be disturbed."_ I ignored his comment, knocked on the door, and heard a stern _"Enter."_ The voice was unmistakably that of the First Sergeant.

I opened the door and stepped into the room. Eight men, mostly officers, were sitting around a table in the room. The First Sergeant was noticeably annoyed by my interruption. _"Moss, this damn well better be important!!"_ he barked. I replied, _"Yes sir, it is. There's a mamasan in barracks 1416 about to give birth at any moment. She's in my bunk."_

A few of the officers around the table choked back a laugh. *"Well, what the hell do you want me to do about your problem?"* he asked trying not to laugh himself. *"I want permission to take the mamasan to her home,"* I said. He refuted, *"Airmen, this is a combat squadron, not an ambulance service. I can't..."* He was interrupted by the CO at the head of the table, *"Sergeant, I don't see anything wrong with his request. Let him take her home where she belongs."*

The First Sergeant looked at me with fire in his eyes, *"Sign out for a jeep and take someone with you. Be back in less than two hours."* I replied, *"Yes sir."* I headed for the door and, almost as an after-thought, the First Sergeant said, *"One more thing Airman... are you the father of the baby?"* I was taken back by his question. I answered in my most commanding voice, *"Absolutely not, sir!"*

Larry Phillips and I got Bá Klaum home before the baby arrived – but just barely. Some neighbors tended to her and we returned to the airbase. I was told the next day that Bá Klaum gave birth to a little girl and both were fine. A Vietnamese teenage girl whose name I never knew substituted for Bá Klaum at the barracks while Bá Klaum recovered. At the beginning of the third week, Bá Klaum returned to work. She nursed her newborn daughter who was carried in a makeshift sling around her neck. She was noticeably proud of her new baby and beamed when she opened the arm sling to allow me to see her new daughter. I gave Bá Klaum some money as a gift for her precious child. Once again, the motherly role of that dear lady surfaced and reinforced my admiration for her.

*****

The two Viet Cong insurgents wearing civilian clothes were on a mission. They were riding through downtown Nha Trang on a motorbike with a host of other travelers – including a military bus on its routine route. Nothing out of the ordinary could have predicted the next scenario. That ordinary morning was about to take a devastating change for bus passengers.

While in route, the motorbike came along side of the bus and the rear rider tossed a primed satchel charge[1] at a side window. The bag clung to the chicken wire that covered the window, and the motorbike turned and sped away. The passengers, realizing what was about to happen, scurried in a near panic away from their looming fate… but not fast enough. The satchel charge exploded blasting a gaping hole in the side of the bus instantly killing one U.S. serviceman and injuring a dozen more.

Once again, the horrors of war reared its ugly head to remind me that anything could happen at anytime! I had taken that identical bus route on many occasions and felt reasonably safe – but now I know that was a false sense of security.

Col. Forster called an impromptu meeting in the dock area for all squadron personnel to discuss the tragic incident. We were shocked to learn the casualty of the bus attack was a member of our squadron. The Colonel made mention of his agony writing the dreadful letter to his wife and family.

He warned everyone not to get lackadaisical about security so to lessen our susceptibility to any terrorist action. His advice was timely but he never mentioned how to carry out his recommendations. With my DEROS nearing, I became paranoid about situations that would heighten my vulnerability to such hostilities. I came really close to being a recluse.

---

[1] A satchel charge was a field-expedient demolition device, typically primed with a non-electric firing system that used a satchel bag containing a suitable amount of explosives. The satchel was sealed shut with string, rope, or tape, while leaving the time fuse and fuse igniter hanging outside. The fuse was lit prior to tossing the charge.

*****

On May 4, 1969, Barbara and I celebrated our one-year wedding anniversary by being twelve thousand miles apart. During our first year of marriage, we had only been together for twenty-two days which included our Hawaiian rendezvous. I arranged for her to receive a dozen roses and I called her via MARS on our special day. The radio connection was weak and it dropped out altogether before our conversation ended. The excitement we both shared wasn't over our anniversary... it was all about me coming home in fifteen days!

*****

Another milestone arrived on May 13. Upon awakening that morning, I immediately tied my short-timer's ribbon into a bow to tell everyone I had *"Single Digit Fidgets!"* Nine more days to go... my FIGMO calendar was almost complete! That day was my last official duty day so I turned in my toolbox, which really made me feel like a short-timer!

The remainder of my time would be spent with administrative and logistic matters – I was entitled to send a limited amount of personal items to my next duty station. I packed my Christmas tree, my two trophies, some clothes, and my electronic correspondence books in what was called "Hold Baggage." The arriving station would hold this baggage until I arrived sometime next month. A GI in the next barracks was quick to buy my electric window fan for ten dollars – a real bargain!

Everything was in order for me to depart except for reconciling with Bá Klaum. She didn't share my excitement about going home – Vietnam was her home and she'd never leave. I wondered just how many servicemen she dealt with in her time as a mamasan and if any had such a special relationship as ours. It would be dreadfully difficult to leave with her being so obstinate – our friendship was important to me and I had to do something to resolve her feelings about me leaving.

*****

I received my Port Call orders and had a nice surprise – my time in-country had been shortened by one day! My orders said to report to the passenger terminal at Cam Ranh Airbase NLT 1000 hours on 20 May, 1969. My *"Freedom Bird"* back to the World was flight G2C4 departing Cam Ranh Airbase at 1430 hours for a CONUS[1] destination! That was sweet music to my ears! I shared the good news with Barbara in a letter and asked her to check airline connections for me from Seattle to Atlanta. It was hard to believe that it was really happening.

*****

In retrospect, the past year had flown by – I suspect that was due to a persistent work schedule which didn't allow time to grind to a halt. I felt like I had done a lot of growing up in terms of facing adversities, enduring attacks, witnessing the anguish of a war-torn country fighting desperately for its freedom, and being separated from my loved ones.

I had done some really stupid things, none of which with lasting consequences. I made an unexpected heart connection with Bá Klaum whom I admired with unconditional respect. I tried to make the best of every situation, and I received some undeserved accolades from my Airman Proficiency Report and two lofty recognitions from PACAF. One thing was for sure… I was ready to leave Vietnam and go home to my bride!

---

[1] Continental United States

Chapter 12

Going Home!

*"And in the end, it's not the year in your life
that counts. It's the life in your year."*
Abraham Lincoln

The months of waiting were over – my time in Vietnam was finished and I was going home. It was a time of mixed feelings because I was leaving a familiar way of life in exchange for another. There was absolutely no doubt I longed to go home... but leaving my cocoon of refuge was a bit daunting. I fully realized I needed to close this chapter of my life and put it behind me... a whole new and glorious lifestyle awaited me back home. The fact I had a darling wife waiting for me on the other side of the world brightened my outlook immensely.

As most people predicted, the year passed incredibly fast. Fortunately, I had endured my time unscathed except for some annoying sunburn and a brief kidney ailment. I had managed to survive the incessant heat, mortar attacks, mosquitoes, FCFs, barbed wire, and 33 Beer. It had been an incredible experience!

On my final night at Nha Trang, I stood outside and peered into the cloudless sky to see a beautiful crescent new moon that accompanied the silent flares. When I finally climbed in my bunk, I wish I hadn't sold my window fan so soon – the heat was maddening which made for an uncomfortable night. In addition to that, I was so psyched up over leaving that I had trouble sleeping.

Another concern I had was a mortar attack on my last night[1]. Thankfully, it didn't happen.

The following morning, the full realization hit me – I was leaving Nha Trang…that day! I stood briefly outside the barracks and took a nostalgic look around the squadron. It was a typical morning with servicemen bustling around and passing jeeps creating clouds of dust on the roadway. An O-1F Bird Dog lifted off the runway, turned left, and passed directly overhead carrying a full load of rockets. I recognized the tail number as one I had flown backseat during an FCF. The aircraft disappeared beyond the mountain range and I whispered a prayer for its safe return.

Everything, even the mundane occurrences, took on a special significance. I had slept in my bunk for the last time, worked on my last aircraft, played the Chapel organ for the last time, had my last in-country haircut, wrote my last letter, received my final letter[2], and lunch would be my final meal at the chow hall. The flight to Cam Ranh Airbase was scheduled to depart at 1800 hours.

The final item on my list was to turn in my battle gear – the items that provided me with a sense of protection throughout the past year. In one way, I was glad to get rid of the gear… but in another strange way, I felt a sentimental attachment to my steel helmet and flak vest because of all the long nights we endured together. I arrived at the equipment issue warehouse to find the wiry tech sergeant long gone – a staff sergeant now manned the counter. He pulled my receipt for my gear and checked in all my items. I noticed the issue date of May 23, 1968… almost one year to the day.

---

[1] A total of 1,448 servicemen were killed on their last day in Vietnam.
[2] A grand total of three hundred-fifty letters!

A lingering and troublesome issue I had to resolve before leaving was to reconcile my relationship with Bá Klaum. She might not be willing to change her stance, but I certainly could convey my feelings for our friendship over the past year. At the last moment, I decided to confront her directly and hope for the best.

As usual I found her ironing in the rear of the barracks with her newborn asleep in the arm sling. As I approached her, she looked up and saw me but immediately looked down at her ironing, apparently still sulking. I noticed the laundry mark on my fatigues that she put there long ago.

I quietly stood in front of her hoping she'd look up. Finally I said to her, *"GI di-di Hôm nay*[1]*."* She replied in a few words I didn't understand. I then said, *"Bá Klaum numba one mamasan!"* I saw a brief hint of a smile on her face and she said without looking up, *"GI dinky dau"* which implied I was crazy. She had called me nothing else than "GI" throughout our relationship – she probably never knew my name.

I called her name again but she continued to ignore me. In desperation, I reached down and placed my fingertips under her dainty chin and raised her head. She looked at me through teary eyes and I said, *"Good-bye Bá Klaum."* She replied, almost in a whisper, *"Bye GI."* She blinked her small eyes and tears streamed down both cheeks. I bent down, wiped her face with my handkerchief, and whispered softly, *"Thank you."* She had said good-bye to me and that was what I needed to hear. I wanted to give her a hug but I feared I might hurt her baby, so I grasped both of her small hands and gave them a gentle squeeze. I gave her the

---

[1] GI leave today

remaining Piaster I had in my wallet which amounted to less than twenty dollars. I stood up and walked away, never to see Bá Klaum again.

I picked up my duffle bag and stepped outside just in time to hear the loudspeakers play "Retreat" at 1700 hours as the flags were lowered near headquarters. I stood at attention and faced the flags. I held a motionless salute until the bugle call ended. What a fitting way to bid farewell to Nha Trang.

I boarded the C-7 *Caribou* for the brief flight to Cam Ranh with a sense of closure with Bá Klaum. I now had little remorse in leaving especially knowing that a great homecoming was in store for me in a few short hours. I had arranged to stay overnight with Gary Howell at Cam Ranh and the following morning, report to the passenger terminal for my flight home.

Gary greeted me at the terminal and we headed for his hootch on the far side of the airbase – the extra cot was still available. That evening following supper, Gary declared that I was deserving of a send-off from Vietnam and the hootch's occupants threw a party on my behalf. Music blared from stereo speakers and two prominent guests at the festivities were Jim Beam and Jack Daniel. No sooner than my glass got the least bit empty, someone would promptly refill it to the top with more spirits. Apparently the primary intent for the party was to inebriate the guest of honor – they were successful! I crashed on the cot and the last thing I remember saying to Gary was, *"Howell, if I miss my flight tomorrow because of this, Barbara is gonna be mad as hell!"* I then lapsed into a state of oblivion.

I wasn't sure what woke me the next morning – it was either the heat or my throbbing headache... or both! Gary half-heartedly apologized for the previous night and said it didn't take much booze to get me plastered. We ate some breakfast at the chow hall and I must have downed a gallon of coffee to thwart my hangover. He told me to relax and he'd make sure I got to the passenger terminal in plenty of time for my flight. I took a shower and put on my khaki travel uniform. As a final act of closure, I discarded my jungle fatigues in a trash receptacle with the feeling of "good riddance." I removed my short timer's ribbon to save it as a memento of my experience[1]. Gary drove me to the passenger terminal, and we said our good byes.

The passenger terminal hadn't changed much in a year – the same looking crowd of servicemen was there. I checked in my duffle bag and insured my name was on the passenger manifest for the flight home. I turned in all my MPC except for a few notes I wanted to retain as a keepsake[2]. It felt so good having real money again.

A Seaboard World Airline taxied to the tarmac and in a short

while a crowd of servicemen began to exit the plane and walk single file to the passenger terminal. Amid the newcomers was a "mosquito winged" Airman who reminded me of another Airman who arrived a year before. A flood of memories filled my head.

---

[1]   Today, my short-timers ribbon is in a shadow box along with other Vietnam mementos.

[2]   After the exchange, GIs were restricted to the passenger terminal to prevent greenback dollars from infiltrating the Black Market.

The commercial DC-8 aircraft was dubbed *"Freedom Bird"* by returning GIs. Flight C2G4 would depart at 1400 hours nonstop to Kokota Airbase in Japan and then continue to McChord AFB in Washington.

The flight was called and the jovial swarm of servicemen filed onboard looking a great deal different than the previous group who just arrived. Once again, I made a conscious effort to remember the precise moment my foot stepped off Vietnam soil. A cheer spontaneously erupted from the crowd when the aircraft lifted off the runway.

I was seated on the right side next to a window, and after the cheers subsided, everything became still and quiet. The drone of the engines was soothing and I was overcome with dreariness – probably due to the party the previous night. I drifted off to sleep and dreamt about loading rockets on a Bird Dog. It would take a while for my subconscious to rid itself of Vietnam… to leave a place was one thing – to forget it was certainly another[1].

We landed at Kokota Airbase in Japan after dark, and we disembarked the aircraft to a passenger holding area. The place had some duty-free shops inside and I looked for Seiko wristwatches as a gift for my Dad and for Barbara's Dad. I found the wristwatches I wanted and began to make the purchase. The transaction was halted because the shop would not accept U.S. currency – only Japanese Yen. The shop proprietor pointed to an exchange window where I obtained the necessary Yen to make the purchase. The total price for the two wristwatches was less then fifty U.S. dollars.

---

[1] Four decades later, I still have occasional dreams about Vietnam.

The flight was called and we re-boarded the aircraft. The pilot announced over the cabin speakers that Kokota had insufficient fuel available for the nonstop flight to the U.S. mainland so we would make an intermediate stopover in Anchorage, Alaska. This deviation hardly upset anyone – just as long as we were headed home.

We departed Japan and began the long flight across the North Pacific Ocean, once again crossing the International Dateline. Traveling east allowed us to lose time as we flew – which made up for the time gained a year ago. It was hard to comprehend.

In a preoccupied and pensive mood, I stared out the window into the night – the darkness punctuated by the flashing wingtip light. It was hard to believe that I was actually experiencing what I had been envisioning for twelve months. I wondered if Barbara or my parents would see a noticeable change in me. What does a year in Vietnam do to a person other than make him appreciate the menial things that occur in his everyday life? Would they notice a callousness or personal intolerance about my demeanor… or would they see a more sympathetic and understanding person emerge? I wrestled with these things until my mind was snarled with speculation and conjecture. I closed my eyes and tried not to think about any of these things. The moment was so surreal – only a few more hours and I'd be home!

We flew into daylight long before arriving at Anchorage. The view of the snowcapped mountains was majestic and a welcomed sight compared to the equatorial heat in which I was accustomed. We landed at Anchorage International Airport and were once again on U.S. soil! As I stepped off the aircraft, I gasped at the nippy air – being chilled was totally foreign to me.

Once inside the terminal, I made a beeline to a payphone and made a collect call to Atlanta. Barbara's Mom accepted the collect call, but she thought it was a MARS call and kept saying *"Over"* until I told her I was calling from Alaska. She was thrilled and said Barbara had gone to the store and wouldn't return for some time. I told her of the  expected arrival time in Seattle and when they needed to meet me at the Atlanta airport. There was a line of GIs waiting to use the phone so I cut short the connection and told her I'd see her real soon!

The flight from Anchorage to McChord AFB seemed like an eternity. We finally landed and the whole crowd cheered again when we touched the runway. I went through an expedited out-processing and claimed my duffle bag. A line of taxicabs awaited our arrival and I crammed into a cab with four other servicemen. I sat in the center seat next to the driver who already knew our destination – SeaTac International Airport.

The route to the airport was via the freeway and the trip was a bit unnerving for me – I wasn't accustomed to all the traffic and fast driving. Then it happened – another taxi ahead of us made a sudden stop and our driver screeched his brakes…but not quick enough. We collided with the other vehicle and I was thrust forward banging my knee against the dashboard. The other occupants were shaken but none hurt. The collision wasn't major and after the drivers swapped information, we continued to the airport. When I got out of the taxi, my knee was sore and I had a noticeable limp due to the accident. I hobbled immediately to the ticket counter and purchased a one-way ticket to Atlanta. It was a Northwest Orient flight – nonstop to Chicago where I connected with a Delta flight to Atlanta. I got the gate assignment and began limping to the gate area.

I didn't notice the raggedy hippy following me down the concourse until he began arrogantly making slurs and innuendos directed toward me. I supposed he was a war protestor and wanted to lash out at anyone who was associated with Vietnam. I ignored his remarks which apparently annoyed him because he became really vocal and belligerent while trying to make a disturbance. When he loudly called me a *"baby killer,"* that was enough. I abruptly stopped and turned around to find him not more than two steps behind me. He had long stringy dark hair and dressed in jeans with holes in the knees, sandals, and a black sweatshirt depicting a peace symbol.

I told him sternly to back off and he refuted, *"I was right... you are a baby killer!"* Then he brashly spit in my face. In an instant, he found himself sprawled over a row of seats clutching his bloody nose[1]. He began to rant at a nearby security guard who had witnessed the incident, *"He attacked me! He broke my nose! You saw what happened...you're my witness. I'm gonna press charges and that sonofabitch baby killer is going to jail!"* I angrily approached him again but the security guard told me to gather my belongings and be on my way. I wiped my face with my handkerchief while staring him in

---

[1] It was years later that I told anyone of this encounter.

the eyes. I then turned and walked away with a limp and a throbbing right hand – both attained since returning stateside.

I boarded the commercial flight and found an empty seat toward the back of the plane. I sat down and took several deep breaths with my eyes closed – I had to ease my nerves from my encounter with that jerk. All I wanted to do was to get home... not a single thought about Vietnam entered my mind.

During the flight, an elderly woman beside me asked if I was returning from Vietnam. How did she know that? I replied, *"Yes mam... I just got back and I'm heading home to my wife in Atlanta!"* She asked, *"So tell me...are things as bad there as the TV news says it is?"* That sounded like a loaded question so I answered carefully, *"I was sorta safe at my location and was spared a lot of the real bad stuff... but I heard stories of some pretty terrible things happening there that I never saw."* That seemed to satisfy her and she then added, *"Well, you try to forget all that and go home to your family. I'm glad you're okay and I appreciate what all you young boys are doing for the country."* I thanked her and we didn't speak again for the remainder of the flight.

The aircraft touched down at the Atlanta Airport and I felt like cheering... but I didn't. Being toward the back, I was among the last of the passengers to exit the plane. My heart was pounding when I entered the gate area of the terminal. I looked intently through the crowd and there she was – my beautiful bride was jumping and waving her hands to get my attention. Mom and Dad were standing with her with huge smiles. I barged through the crowd and Barbara came toward me until we met. I gave her a long tight but silent hug. My eyes filled with tears at the realization I was home and embracing my darling wife. Mom and Dad came over to where we were and I greeted them with more hugs. I then saw something I'd never seen before – Dad was blinking back tears. At that moment, *everyone* had tears! It was a glorious homecoming and it was every bit as wonderful as I had imagined!

I picked up my duffle bag at baggage claim and we all walked outside to the parking lot... all the while I was trying to conceal my limp and my swollen hand. I had another surprise – our new car! It was very sporty and so shiny. I told Barbara, *"You did good... real good!"* Barbara and I sat together in the back seat with Mom and Dad in the front. We headed for their home in Gresham Park, a residential suburb east of Atlanta. The air conditioning felt wonderful!

Mom had prepared the guest bedroom for Barbara and me. When we arrived, I plopped down on the double bed and stretched out – I had been cooped up in an aircraft seat for what seemed like an eternity and the bed felt so good. Later, we all congregated in the family room and had a perfectly delightful time being reunited with all my family. I gave Dad his Seiko watch and he seemed to like it – he put it on his wrist right away. We talked about most everything and I showed everyone my pictures. Mom was the most inquisitive – she wanted to know all the mundane things about my experience. She said my safe return was an answer to her daily prayers – her only child was again safe and sound. I had previously offered God a silent prayer of gratitude for His unwavering protection through many times of trials and tribulations.

That evening following a scrumptious home-cooked fried chicken dinner, Barbara and I sat cuddled up on the couch in the living room. I started to take notice of some of the comforts that I had been denied... things like air conditioning, color television, fresh fruit, carpeting, bread without black specks, and most of all…my wife!

I stepped outside on the patio and heard crickets chirping – something that I hadn't thought about or missed in a year. Two things were strikingly absent – the sound of H&I howitzers and bright flares in the night sky. I peered into the night sky to see the same crescent moon I had seen at Nha Trang two nights before – but now I was on the other side of the planet. Strangely, the earth didn't seem as big as I once thought.

I finally had a sense of closure with my Vietnam year. As atypical as it was, it challenged me to excel and to benefit in terms of insightfulness. Now that it was over, my energy could be directed toward future endeavors with the knowledge that I had endured adversity and emerged a conqueror.

But at that current moment, I was overly occupied with the indescribable yet so magnificent realization that I was experiencing – it could be summed up in three short words: *I was home!!*

EPILOGUE

After twelve long months of separation, Barbara and I finally began our married life together – something that was a daily topic of conservation in our letters. At Nellis AFB, I was granted off-base living privilege and we rented a one-bedroom furnished apartment in North Las Vegas about four miles from the base. On June 11, 1969, I was awarded the Air Force Commendation Medal for my service in Vietnam. Today, that medal along with other Vietnam mementos are displayed in a shadowbox in our family room.

I remained at Nellis AFB for the duration of my active service and received an Honorable Discharge on September 18, 1971 as a Staff Sergeant (E-5). Barbara and I returned home to Atlanta where I gained employment with the Federal Aviation Administration in 1972 and transferred to Maryville, Tennessee in 1977. We raised two sons, both of whom became military officers – the older son a career Naval Officer.

The 21st Tactical Air Support Squadron relocated to Cam Ranh Airbase in October 1969. The final relocation was back to the 377th Airbase Wing at Tan Son Nhut Airbase near Saigon on March 15 1972. It remained at Tan Son Nhut until it was deactivated on February 23, 1973. Aircraft losses while engaged in combat included 41 O-1E/F *Bird Dogs*, 16 O-2A *Skymasters*, and a single OV-10 *Bronco*.

Fulfiling a campaign promise to lessen U.S. involvememt in Vietnam, President Richard M. Nixon began a gradual withdrawal of troops in 1970[1]. The plan, which was called "vietnamization", was to strengthen the South Vietnamese armed forces by equipping it with modern weapons so that they could defend their nation on their own. Sadly, such was not the case.

By March 14, 1975, a major offensive by the North Vietnamese Army prompted South Vietnamese President Nguyen Van Thieu to order a general withdrawal of military forces from the Central Highland area. Instead of an orderly withdrawal, it turned into a panic exodus with thousands of military and civilians fleeing, clogging roads, and creating chaos. Many refugees believed Nha Trang to be a safe haven, and by April 1, 1975, the panic of the retreat reached Nha Trang. The city was quickly abandoned by the South Vietnamese Army, yielding the entire area to the North Vietnamese. The offensive continued southward and on April 3, 1975, North Vietnamese forces captured Cam Ranh Bay and all of its military facilities.

The North Vietnamese aggression continued until April 30, 1975 when the Army overcame all resistance by quickly capturing key buildings and installations in Saigon. A tank crashed through the gates of the Presidential Palace and at 11:30 AM, and the North Vietnamese flag was raised above it. President Duong Văn Minh, who had been president of South Vietnam for only three days, issued his last command, ordering all South Vietnamese troops to lay down their arms. The war was finally over. Saigon was later renamed Ho Chi Minh City.

By 1975 the Vietnamese economy lay in shambles and it would take decades to rebuild. Most of the population of 55 million were

---

[1] By end of 1973, only 50 U.S. servicemen were in Vietnam down from 536,100 only five years previous.

unemployed, impoverished, and suffering from the emotional and physical ramifications of the war. Over 2 million had been killed and 300,000 were reported missing and presumed dead. Many more Vietnamese lost loved ones and family members. By the 1990s, the loss of so many adults made Vietnam one of the youngest nations on earth.

The Vietnam War was extremely costly in terms of both money and lives – more than fifty-eight thousand Americans died and the financial cost to the United States exceeded $150 billion dollars. The war was the longest and most unpopular war in which Americans ever fought. The toll in suffering, sorrow, and national turmoil can never be tabulated. No one ever wants to see America so divided again, and for many of the more than two million American veterans of the war, the wounds of Vietnam will never heal.

General Douglas MacArthur[1] once said:

"Once war is forced upon us, there is no other alternative than to apply every available means to bring it to a swift end. War's very objective is victory – not prolonged indecision. In war, indeed, there can be no substitute for victory."

His words clearly imply that once we are engaged in combat, there must be a firm resolution to win and bring the conflict to a swift end. There were no such plans in Vietnam and the war went on for many years with a tarnished legacy which lingers to this date.

In 1998, my family and I visited the Vietnam War Memorial in Washington DC. The memorial recognizes and honors the men and women who served in one of America's most divisive wars.

---

[1] Douglas MacArthur (1900-1964) was a Five-Star General of the Army.

EPILOGUE

The memorial grew out of a need to heal the nation's wounds as America struggled to reconcile moral differences and political points of view. In fact, the memorial was conceived and designed to make no political statement whatsoever about the war. Born in controversy, the radically simple design of the memorial was originally a school project for a Yale architecture student, twenty-one year old Chinese American Maya Ying Lin.

The Vietnam Veterans Memorial is a place where everyone, regardless of opinion, can come together and remember and honor those who served. By doing so, the memorial has paved the way towards reconciliation and healing, a process that continues today.

The central theme of the wall is closure – the ability to bring closure has been the most remarkable quality of this mending wall. The power comes from the 58,235 names and room for more – all the dead and missing from an entire war. No memorial has ever attempted such a complete commemoration. This black granite edifice is a testimony of how the dead and missing can be more than a memorial.

During my visit I found several familiar names on the Wall, including Sergeant Dumas. Then something happened that I had not anticipated – the wall began to scream at me... all those names took on a face and seemed to be somehow trapped on the other side of the wall. A burning question that confronted me was why my name *wasn't* on the wall. I became overcome with emotion and had to leave in fear of totally losing it. A daunting thought lingered with me – in the not too distant future, those names on the wall will be just that... *names*. One day, nobody will connect those names with a person, a husband, a brother, a son, or ROTC instructor.

EPILOGUE

In September 2000, a special memorial was dedicated to specifically honor all the Air Force Forward Air Controllers who died in Southeast Asia. The memorial is located in the Air Park on Hurlburt Field near Fort Walton Beach, Florida. More than two hundred names adorn the memorial which help explain the words on the monument – *"All Gave Some, But Some Gave All."*

Today, Nha Trang's airport is closed with all civil airline traffic being routed to the new facility at Cam Ranh Airport. However, Nha Trang has become Vietnam's premier beach resort community. A major face-lift in 1995-96, and the opening of two upscale hotels later in 1996, vaulted Nha Trang onto the playing field with places like Phuket, Thailand, and Cancun, Mexico. Today, it's a popular destination for both foreign and domestic tourists. A new aerial gondolier shuttles tourists from the mainland to Hon Tre Island, where several lush resorts are located. In 2008 the Miss Universe Pageant was held at Nha Trang – such lush amenities now available in a former war-torn town continues to boggle my mind.

In retrospect, my experiences in Vietnam were in sharp contrast to my urban upbringing – a naïve product of the 60's era. I was raised in a stable environment by loving and caring Christian parents who provided immunity and isolation from a cruel and spiteful world. Strong core values and ethics became my anchor to fight the ceaseless temptations afforded to the average American soldier in Vietnam. Having a new bride back home also significantly added to my overall mental health. We "spoke" to each other almost daily via precious handwritten letters that were five days old at the reading – all of which we have reread on the

EPILOGUE

40th anniversary of the date of each letter. The promise of a better day when I returned was foremost in our letters.

I treasure my association with Bá Klaum because she helped me realize the human side of the war. Her devotion to her faith, family, and work was truly inspirational and she earned my unconditional admiration. I never expected to grow such a deep heart connection with her, and I have wondered often about her fate. She was a warrior, not in terms of a military soldier, but as a compassionate soul who fought diligently for her heritage and family.

During the time of my Vietnam involvement, I was an unknowing twenty-year old who didn't have an inkling of why we were at war. I felt like it was my duty to serve and do anything I was ordered. Today, with a more mature perspective, I believe the war was a manifestation of several disdained political agendas starting with an innocent decision to "help" a new democratic country defend itself against communism. The circumstances quickly became a political and military quagmire with no avenue of escape. CBS news anchorman Walter Cronkite told the nation that the war was destined to remain deadlocked[1]:

"We have been too often disappointed by the optimism of the American leaders, both in Vietnam and Washington, to have faith any longer in the silver linings they find in the darkest clouds.... For it seems now more certain than ever that the bloody experience of Vietnam is to end in a stalemate. To say that we are mired in stalemate seems the only realistic, yet unsatisfactory conclusion."

---

[1] *"Report from Vietnam"* Walter Cronkite Broadcast, February 27, 1968.

EPILOGUE

I had it pretty good in terms of overall living conditions and physical security as compared with most soldiers serving in Vietnam – and to this day, it's something for which I'm thankful. The mortar attacks I experienced were of no serious consequence and seldom inflicted any substantial damage or causalities – but at the time, the attacks most definitely created episodes of anxiety and fright for me. Fortunately, I didn't bring home any demons or any other deep-seeded memories of unspeakable atrocities as so many Vietnam veterans endured. I've never been plagued with "flashbacks" or nightmares and have sympathy for those who do[1].

I did a lot of growing up in those twelve months. Any type of war can harden the heart and create lifelong calluses. But it can also open your eyes to the abundant blessings from our Creator. Without a doubt, I was afforded protection by a spiritual presence that never abandoned me. Too many occurrences happened that simply couldn't be written off as coincidence. Prayer was also a major player – something I relied on daily.

Am I better off today because of my time in Vietnam? That remains to be determined. I returned from Vietnam with a whole different view of mankind's inhumanities against its own and a deepened appreciation of where I lived and the freedoms I once took for granted. I look back at that year with trepidation knowing how senseless the war actually proved to be.

---

[1] Known as Post Traumatic Stress Disorder or "PTSD," this anxiety disorder can develop after exposure to a terrifying event in which grave physical harm occurred or was threatened. It is a severe and ongoing emotional reaction to an extreme psychological trauma. Reportedly, more than 15% of all male Vietnam veterans (approximately 479,000) have been diagnosed with PTSD.

EPILOGUE

Sadly, all of the expended energy incurred, money spent, bombs dropped, and lives destroyed or lost were for naught. Despite the fact that our military was undefeated on the battlefield, in the end, everything we had fought for was lost. Perhaps the only lesson learned from Vietnam was just that – *a lesson*. History books might tell us otherwise, but we as a nation should never put ourselves in that predicament again.

Bibliography

Tucker, Spencer.   The Encyclopedia of the Vietnam War. Oxford University Press, 2000.

Columbia Encyclopedia, Sixth Edition, Columbia University Press, New York 2001-2004.

A Pocket Guide to Vietnam, DOD PG-21A, U.S. Govt. Printing Office, 1966.

Vietnamese Phrase Book, Holt, Rinehart and Winston, New York, 1966.

Wikipedia, free online encyclopedia.

Harvey, Frank. Air War – Vietnam. Bantam Books, 1967.

Davis, Kenneth C. Don't Know Much About© American History. Avon Books, 1995.

Brokaw, Tom.   BOOM! Random House 2007.

Scruggs, Jan C. The American Patriot, Vietnam Veterans Memorial Fund 2005.

Kranz, Gene. Failure is Not an Option, Berkley Books New York May 2001.

About the Author

Originally from Atlanta, Georgia, Dean Moss and his wife Barbara relocated to Maryville, Tennessee in 1977, the result of a job transfer with the Federal Aviation Administration. There they raised their two sons, Scott and David.

Dean became involved in several volunteer community programs and church related activities such as Little League Baseball, missionary trips to Haiti and Africa, and *Turkeys in the Straw* – a musical group that performs at retirement homes and assisted living centers. Most recently, he became president of the Community Food Connection – an organization that distributes food to needy families.

Perhaps Dean's most fervent passion (other than his grandchildren) is Scouting. He has served as a Scoutmaster since 1985 during which time he led scout troops to the *National Jamboree* three times, served as course director for *Wood Badge*, and was awarded the prestigious *Silver Beaver* recognition. Both of his sons are Eagle Scouts and he has personally awarded forty-two Eagles thus far during his time as Scoutmaster.

He is now retired from the Federal Aviation Administration after thirty-seven years as a systems specialist for electronic navigational systems. He enjoys reading, writing, gardening, woodworking, music, astronomy, and spoiling his five grandchildren.

Printed in the United States
by Baker & Taylor Publisher Services